QUOTIDIANA

Q U O

TIDIANA

PATRICK MADDEN

University of Nebraska Press
Lincoln and London

Acknowledgments for previously
published material appear on
pages xiv–xv, which constitute an
extension of the copyright page.

Library of Congress
Cataloging-in-Publication Data
Madden, Patrick, 1971–
Quotidiana / Patrick Madden.
p. cm. ISBN 978-0-8032-2296-0
(cloth : alkaline paper)
1. Essays. I. Title.
PS3613.A28355Q68 2010
814'.6 – dc22   2009032888

Set in Arno by Bob Reitz.
Designed by Nathan Putens.

For Karina, eternamente

From the most ordinary, commonplace,
familiar things, if we could put them
in their proper light, can be formed the
greatest miracles of nature and the most
wondrous examples.

MONTAIGNE "Of Experience"

The most common actions — a
walk, a talk, solitude in one's own
orchard — can be enhanced and lit up
by the association of the mind.

VIRGINIA WOOLF "Montaigne"

Consider the circumvolutions of the
human mind, where no short or direct
routes exist.

JOSÉ SARAMAGO *Essay on Blindness*

CONTENTS

List of Illustrations *xi*

Acknowledgments *xiii*

The Infinite Suggestiveness
of Common Things *1*

Laughter *11*

Remember Death *29*

Garlic *61*

Ego Vici Mundum *72*

Gravity and Distance *81*

Panis Angelicus *94*

Asymptosy *111*

Singing *138*

Hepatitis *155*

Finity *164*

ILLUSTRATIONS

1. *Laughing Kookabura*, unknown artist, circa 1790, watercolor 15

2. *Democritus*, William Blake, 1789, illustration 16

3. *Abraham and the Three Angels*, unknown artist, *Psalter of St. Louis*, 13th century, manuscript illumination 23

4. Rush ticket stub, unknown computer, 1991, ink on cardstock, courtesy of the author 35

5. *Vanitas Still Life*, Jacques de Gheyn, 1603, oil on wood 37

6. *The Physician*, Hans Holbein the Younger, 1538, woodcut 38

7. *The Cemetery*, Hans Holbein the Younger, 1538, woodcut 39

8. *The Meeting of Paul and Anthony*, Matthias Grünewald, Isenheim altarpiece, 1512, oil on wood 40

9. *Jerome in His Study*, Albrecht Dürer, 1514, engraving 41

10. *Thomas the Apostle*, Raffaello Schiaminossi, 1602, engraving 43

11. *Death of Seneca*, Jacques-Louis David, 1773, oil on canvas 51

12. *Witchcraft at Salem Village*, either F. O. C. Darley, William L. Shepard, or Granville Perkins, 1876, engraving 53

13. *Temptation of St. Anthony*, Matthias Grünewald, Isenheim altarpiece, 1512, oil on wood 54

14. *The Ambassadors*, Hans Holbein the Younger, 1533, oil on oak 55

15. Mercado Modelo, Montevideo, photograph by Uber Cabrera, 2009, courtesy of the photographer 63

16. *Allium Sativum*, unknown artist, *Lectures on the Elements of Botany*, Anthony Todd Thompson, 1822, drawing 68

17. Grandmothers of the Plaza de Mayo, Buenos Aires, photograph by Jeffrey Shumway, 2008, courtesy of the photographer 75

18. Ego Vici Mundum, Catedral Metropolitana, Buenos Aires, photograph by Jeffrey Shumway, 2008, courtesy of the photographer 78

19. Catedral Metropolitana, Buenos Aires, photograph by Jeffrey Shumway, 2008, courtesy of the photographer 80

20. *Michel de Montaigne*, Edmond Boulenaz, 1893, engraving *81*

21. *The Trial of Abraham's Faith*, Gustave Doré, 1866, engraving *92*

22. Madden family, unknown photographer, circa 1942, courtesy of the author *97*

23. *The Witch of Agnesi*, unknown diagrammer, *Instituzioni analitiche ad uso della gioventù italiana*, Maria Gaetana Agnesi, 1748, drawing *115*

24. Jeffrey Dahmer, photograph by Gary Porter, 1991 *129*

25. Patrick Madden, 2003, photograph courtesy of the author *129*

26. John Schneider, unknown photographer, circa 1982, courtesy of Scott Romine *129*

27. Patrick and Sara Madden, photograph by Daniel Madden, 2005, courtesy of the photographer *129*

28. David Pirner, photograph by Barry Brecheisen, 1998 *129*

29. Patrick Madden, 2003, photograph courtesy of the author *129*

30. Russell Crowe, photograph by Thomas Schulz, 2005, courtesy of the photographer *129*

31. Ace Frehley, unknown videographer, 1979, video still *130*

32. Patrick Madden on the staff of the Whippany Park High School newspaper, unknown photographer, 1988, courtesy of the author *130*

33. Alex Lifeson, unknown videographer, 1984, video still *130*

34. Plate XIV, William Blake, *The Book of Job*, 1825, engraving *146*

35. Hepatitis A virus, electron micrograph by Betty Partin, Centers for Disease Control, 1976 *158*

36. *Still Life with Grapes*, Edward Deakin, 1888, oil on canvas *164*

37. *The Angel Staying the Arm of Abraham*, Giovanni Battista Franco, 16th century, engraving *173*

38. *Archimedes Is Killed by a Soldier*, Jost Amman, 16th century, woodcut *175*

39. *Archimedes' Lever*, Whiting and Branston, *Mechanic's Magazine*, 1824, woodcut *180*

40. *The Fall of Man*, Hugo Van Der Goes, 1479, oil on panel *186*

41. *Amedeo Avogadro*, C. Sentier, 1851, drawing *188*

ACKNOWLEDGMENTS

Above all, I thank the members of my family — Karina, Pato, Adi, Sara, Dani, Marcos, and James — who have supported me in all my foolish pursuits. They have my undying love. I also thank my mother and father — Liz and Pat — and my siblings — Kathleen, David, and Dan — as well as my in-laws — Uber, Teresa, Fernando, Graciela, David, Valeria, Ivan, Thiago, Tiziana, and Augusto.

If I have learned anything about writing, it is because of my friends — John Bennion, David Lazar, Michael Danko, Shannon Lakanen, Desirae Matherly, and Brian Doyle. I have greatly benefited from the kindnesses of Eduardo Galeano, David Hamilton, Michael Martone, Dinty Moore, and Philip Zaleski. I likewise am blessed by my association with so many fine people — faculty, staff, and students — at Ohio University and Brigham Young University.

My essay habit has been generously supported by the J. William Fulbright Commission (special thanks to Patricia Vargas in Montevideo); Brigham Young University's Graduate School, College of Humanities, and English Department (special thanks to John Rosenberg and Ed Cutler); the Utah Humanities Council; and Ohio University's College of Arts and Sciences and English Department. I appreciate the kind recognition afforded me by the Association of Writers and Writing Programs, *Western Humanities Review*, the Association for Mormon Letters, the Utah Arts Council, *The Best American Spiritual Writing*, and *The Best Creative Nonfiction*.

The essay form, from its earliest examples, relies on the integration of others' creations. I am indebted to many authors, musicians, photographers, painters, etc. for their unwitting contributions to this book, but I especially thank those witting artists who've granted me their permission to use their work: Mark Halliday, Neil Peart, and Jeffrey Shumway. Kevin J. Anderson helped me get permission to use so many Rush lyrics. Scott Romine helped me get permission for the image of John Schneider. Lara Burton helped me find and scan most of the images included herein. I've used the King James Version of the Bible for all biblical quotations.

Of course, I humbly thank the good people at the University of Nebraska Press. Ladette Randolph and Kristen Elias Rowley started things off wonderfully, and their fine work was continued by Sue Breckenridge, Carolyn Einspahr, Tish Fobben, Acacia Lemke, Kim Mahrt, Cara Pesek, Erika Rippeteau, Alison Rold, Sara Springsteen, and Rhonda Winchell. I am impressed by the beautiful typography and design work of Bob Reitz and Nathan Putens. It has been a great pleasure to work with all of them.

Pages 1–204 constitute an extension of these acknowledgments. To those whose names appear within this book (names have not been changed; there are no innocents), I offer much deserved gratitude for making my essays possible.

Finally, I would also like to thank the editors of the journals and magazines where the following essays were first published:

"Laughter" first appeared in *North Dakota Quarterly* 69.1 (Winter 2002); an edited version was published as "On Laughing" in *Portland Magazine* 25.3 (Fall 2006), then again as "On Laughing" in *The Best American Spiritual Writing 2007* (Boston: Houghton Mifflin, 2007), and then, with different edits, as "On Laughter" in BYU *Magazine* 63.2 (Spring 2009).

"Garlic" first appeared as "Thoughts occasioned by my father-in-law, garlic, and Montevideo's Mercado Modelo" in

Fourth Genre 9.1 (Spring 2007); an edited version was published as "A Hint of Garlic" in *Portland Magazine* 29.1 (Spring 2010).

"Ego Vici Mundum" first appeared in *Quarterly West* 64 (Spring/Summer 2007); an edited version was published as "A Sudden Pull behind the Heart" in *Portland Magazine* 26.3 (Fall 2007), then again as "A Sudden Pull behind the Heart" in *The Best Creative Nonfiction*, vol. 2 (New York: Norton, 2008).

"Gravity and Distance" first appeared in *Mississippi Review* 8.2 (Spring 2002).

"Panis Angelicus" first appeared in *Western Humanities Review* 62.2 (Spring 2008).

"Asymptosy" first appeared in *Hotel Amerika* 6.1 (Spring 2008).

"Hepatitis" first appeared in *The Laurel Review* 39.2 (Summer 2005).

"Finity" first appeared in *The Iowa Review* 38.1 (Spring 2008).

QUOTIDIANA

The Infinite Suggestiveness of Common Things

> A quick ear and eye, an ability to discern the infinite
> suggestiveness of common things, a brooding meditative
> spirit, are all that the essayist requires.
>
> ALEXANDER SMITH "On the Writing of Essays"

A few years ago, a curmudgeonly professor, a guy who was
always giving me a hard time about my genre, asked, "What
will you do when you run out of experiences to write about?"
He wanted me to admit that I'd have to turn to fiction or suffer
the ignominy of rewriting the same handful of exciting experi
ences I'd had in my life.

I answered him by saying something about having children,
how they were a renewable source of writing material, with
their quirks and insights and inscrutable ways. And it's true:
kids are full of wisdom that you can write from. Not too long
ago, my oldest daughter, who speaks both English and Spanish,
misunderstood the Paul McCartney song "Coming Up" to say
"*Caminar* like a flower," which is, "Walk like a flower," which I
like better than "Walk like an Egyptian," at least. And just the
other day, another daughter, whom I'd just put to bed, grew
impatient waiting for me to bring her a tissue. When I finally
appeared, she pointed to her nose and explained, "I put the
booger back." At least she didn't wipe it on the blanket.

The essay is an open, leisurely form, somewhat allergic to adventure, certainly opposed to sensationalism. Even Montaigne, when he encounters a "monstrous child," a traveling freak show exploited by his uncle for profit, turns his thoughts to a subversion of common notions of "natural," with barely a mention of the exotic scene he's witnessed. During my first extended encounters with the essay, I was struck (dumbstruck, moonstruck) by those authors who wrote from seemingly insignificant, overlooked, transient things, experiences, and ideas, who were able to find within their everyday, unexceptional lives inspiration for essaying. What is it Phillip Lopate says in the introduction to *The Art of the Personal Essay*? He says, "The essayist . . . aligns himself with what is traditionally considered a female perspective, in its appreciation of sentiment, dailiness, and the domestic."

While children are certainly part of the daily and domestic, that's not how I should have answered my antagonistic amigo. Would that I had known then Alexander Smith, the nineteenth-century Scottish "spasmodic" poet whose essays, recently, have been a revelation to me. Here is *trepverter, l'esprit de l'escalier*,[1] if I've ever known it. Professor Thayer, this is what I would say to you now:

> The essay-writer has no lack of subject-matter. He has the day that is passing over his head; and, if unsatisfied with that, he has the world's six thousand years to depasture his gay or serious humour upon. I idle away my time here, and I am finding new subjects every hour. Everything I see or hear is an essay in bud. The world is everywhere whispering essays, and one need only be the world's amanuensis.

Because I only recently learned the word *amanuensis*, I thought I'd allow you, dear reader, a bit of my own process.

As often happens, I learned the word then heard it again several times in the following week. Shortly after my first contact, in the above quote from Smith's "On the Writing of Essays," I met it again in my friend Stephen Tuttle's short story "Amanuensis," about a disappeared junior high school biology teacher with a scale model of the town in his basement. Then, as I studied the biography of essayist Vernon Lee, a.k.a. Violet Paget, I learned that she had acted as an amanuensis for her sickly older brother, poet Eugene Hamilton-Lee. By then, of course, I had looked it up in several dictionaries, but even before I knew what it meant, I liked the word and knew it was important. Just look at it: *amanuensis*. Is that French? It has as many vowels as consonants. It's an anagram for "sun amnesia" and "sane animus" and "manna issue" (which all sound wonderfully fascinating, don't they?). But what does it mean? You may be disappointed to learn that an amanuensis is a secretary or stenographer, "one employed to write from dictation or to copy manuscript." But if you think instead of a cloistered monk toiling by candlelight at some glorious copywork, taking pains not just to write but to draw letters, to illustrate, to infuse his work with spirit and reverence, then you will be closer to the notions the word conveys to me.

Amanuensis is a fine word, but my favorite word is *quotidian*, a word I learned later in life, from Spanish, and which I pined for, eagerly sought in English, until one magical day I found it. Let's back up: in the early 1990s I was living in Uruguay as a missionary, picking up Spanish from conversations and signs, and I kept hearing the phrase *la vida cotidiana*. This, I surmised or discovered, meant "everyday life." But the choice of words seemed so elegant, and that adjective, *cotidiana*, so unlike what it meant, that I fell in love. What a word to mean "mundane, everyday, common, etc."! So beautiful, so seemingly opposite its meaning!

When I returned to New Jersey, one of my first tasks was to find this *cotidiana* in English. Knowing that the French influence on English left a rich legacy of Latinate words, which vary from their Spanish cognates by a letter or two, to the dictionary I went. From the dictionary I came, disappointed. There was no such word, not even in the library's multivolume OED.

Meanwhile, I began my graduate studies in English, hoping to learn how to write, to become an essayist. Then I learned that essays were not stories, did not focus on great adventures or recoveries, were not extraordinary in their subject matter at all. Essayists are keen observers of the overlooked, the ignored, the seemingly unimportant. They can make the mundane resplendent with their meditative insights.

Then one day, as I was leafing through the dictionary —

> Researches, however great or small, [are] great pleasures
> in themselves, full of serendipity; I have rarely paged
> through one of my dictionaries . . . without my eye
> lighting, along the way, on words more beautiful than a
> found fall leaf.
>
> WILLIAM GASS "In Defense of the Book"

— my eye alighted on the word I had been searching for all these years, the word I had hoped for, had almost wished into existence: *quotidian*, with a Q. This was a revelation.

Of course, I then began to read about quotidian writings and concerns in essays and essays on essays, and I began to doubt my own awareness of the world around me. Surely this word had crossed my path before, in other readings, other essays; and yet, maybe not. Perhaps *quotidian* was absent from my life until my need for it became great enough.

And maybe simply knowing the word made me more aware of the world, more open to the miracles drifting by.

> The fastidious habits of polished life generally incline us to reject, as incapable of interesting us, whatever does not present itself in a graceful shape of its own, and a ready-made suit of ornaments. But some of the plainest weeds become beautiful under the microscope. It is the benevolent provision of nature, that in proportion as you feel the necessity of extracting interest from common things, you are enabled to do so.
>
> LEIGH HUNT "On Washerwomen"

One day as I sat at my bedroom computer, writing who-knowswhat, Adriana, then almost three months old, began to laugh behind me on the bed. I turned to see what she was laughing at but could find nothing. Thankfully, I recognized the world whispering, put fingers to keyboard, let the ideas collaborate and grow.

That daughter is now ten years old, and that essay may well be the first good thing I ever wrote. So maybe the value of children, from a writerly standpoint, coincides with the value of the quotidian. Children may awaken us to the marvels slipping past us, almost unnoticed. Scott Russell Sanders, who writes a mean quotidian essay himself, spoke to this in a 1997 Lannan Foundation interview with Bernard Cooper:

> We sleepwalk through most of our lives . . . and . . . every once in a while something happens . . . outside ourselves that forces us to pay attention in a new way, or something happens inside us that enables us to pay attention in a new way. And we suddenly realize that the world is so much richer, and more magnificent, and more wonderful than we had felt for a long time. Not to sentimentalize . . . , but

I think children live much more continuously in a state of awareness of the miraculousness of existence.

I want a genre that allows for the staid, mundane life of a loafer, that reaches for new connections, that recognizes "the world in a grain of sand" (Blake). Of course, to stick to surfaces, to slither hither and yon but never move beyond the everyday, that would be . . . superficial, suicidal. A successful commonplace essay will gather memories and researches, attach ideas and stories to build upward, toward meaning. Again, Alexander Smith:

> [The essayist] lifts a pebble from the ground, and puts it aside more carefully than any gem; and on a nail in a cottage-door he will hang the mantle of his thought. . . . He finds his way into the Elysian fields through portals the most shabby and commonplace. . . . Let him take up the most trivial subject, and it will lead him away to the great questions over which the serious imagination loves to brood — fortune, mutability, death.

This is not to say that the essay can't allow for some extraordinary experience — it is, as Phillip Lopate says, a "wonderfully tolerant form" — but I am inclined to agree with Theodor Adorno that "the bad essay tells stories about people instead of elucidating the matter at hand." I prefer the intellectual surprises wrought from "render[ing] the transient eternal" (Adorno again), the essay I halfway recognize as containing my "own discarded thoughts" (Emerson) or wish I had been observant and curious enough to see. So does Joseph Epstein:

> I prefer when the essay takes a small, very particular subject and, through the force of the essayist's artistically controlled maunderings, touches on unpredictably large

general matters, makes hitherto unexpected conclusions, tells me things I hadn't hitherto known, or reminds me of other things I have always known but never thought to formulate so well.

The Best American Essays 1993

The fact is that essayists have been doing this sort of thing for centuries. Montaigne, who gave us the name for the form and its first, best examples, proclaimed repeatedly the tenet of writing from ordinary things:

> Of the most ordinary, common, and known things, could we but find out their light, the greatest miracles of nature might be formed, and the most wondrous examples.

"Of Experience"

Centuries later, under the influence of the master, William Hazlitt was carried away almost to ecstasy thinking about the infinite possibilities that life offers for thought and writing:

> It is the very extent of human life, the infinite number of things contained in it, its contradictory and fluctuating interests, the transition from one situation to another, the hours, months, years spent in one fond pursuit after another [that], baffling the grasp of our actual perception, make it slide from our memory. . . . What canvas would be big enough to hold its striking groups, its endless subjects! . . . What a huge heap, a "huge, dumb heap," of wishes, thoughts, feelings, anxious cares, soothing hopes, loves, joys, friendships, it is composed of! How many ideas and trains of sentiment, long and deep and intense, often pass through the mind in only one day's thinking or reading, for instance!

"On the Past and Future"

You begin to sense the dizzying possibilities inherent in such a childlike curiosity, the dangers of noticing everything all the time, yet this is a valuable perspective to have, a useful practice to know, for teachers and writers alike. When I have taught the "personal narrative" in freshman composition courses — before I knew what I know now — students inevitably sought their most dramatic, easily significant experiences. For the majority of them, this translated to tales of loss or conquest. Grandparents died; girlfriends broke up with boyfriends; young athletes were nearly cut from school sports teams only to rise up and win a starting spot in the squad, then, preferably, to make the winning shot in the state championships. But my students were unable to write beyond clichés, received ideas, or meanings gathered largely, I presume, from movies and sit-coms. They were force-fitting their experiences to preexisting legends. They were stifling their own thinking in order to match up. Sir Joshua Reynolds, an eighteenth-century British painter who portrayed some of our early essayists (Johnson, Burke, Goldsmith, Sterne), once said, "There is no expedient to which a man will not resort in order to avoid the real effort of thinking." Thomas Edison had this saying framed in every room of his West Orange laboratories.

David Shields is of this mind:

> The world exists. Why recreate it? I want to think about it, try to understand it. . . . I want a literature built entirely out of contemplation and revelation. . . . The real story isn't the drama of what happens; it's what we're thinking about while nothing, or very little, is happening.
>
> "Reality Hunger: A Manifesto"

Writing from the everyday, straining toward new connection, new meaning, is not necessarily easy, but even at its worst, it beats writing banalities as if they were revelation. It is also a stay against the perfidious notion that I, or you, or they, are inherently interesting or important to a world of strangers. Our minds, on the other hand, may offer somewhat of interest to coexplore.

In an interview with Joseph Cuomo, W. G. Sebald gave these matter-of-fact instructions, a kind of play-by-play of the essaying process:

> As you walk along, you find things . . . by the wayside or you buy a brochure written by a local historian which is in a tiny little museum somewhere . . . and in that you find odd details that lead you somewhere else, and so it's a form of unsystematic searching. . . . So you then have a small amount of material and you accumulate things, . . . and one thing takes you to another, and you make something out of these haphazardly assembled materials. And, as they have been assembled in this random fashion, you have to strain your imagination in order to create a connection between . . . things. If you look for things that are like the things that you have looked for before, then, obviously, they'll connect up. But they'll only connect up in an obvious sort of way, which actually isn't, in terms of writing something new, very productive. You have to take heterogeneous materials in order to get your mind to do something that it hasn't done before.

So let's think more, ponder, wonder, meander, maunder. Despite appearances to the contrary, despite the clamor and clang of true-life sensationalism in every medium, quotidian essays are being written and published all the time. They're an antidote to the harried hullabaloo of — what? — talk shows? tabloids? the madding crowd? And so I (and my friends, known and unknown) continue this quiet labor, stopping to smell the roses, suspicious that the tree falling in the forest *does*

The Infinite Suggestiveness 9

make a sound, the cat in the box might as well be alive. The exercise of writing from the infinite suggestiveness of common things has proved fruitful for me time and again, with essays sparked by considerations of garlic, diaper changing, washing grapes, a chipped tooth, and others. I'm addicted to that world's whisper.

And in case you were wondering, that curmudgeonly professor who likes to bust my chops: his latest book is a memoir, a kind of catalog of the everyday life of a Mormon boy in 1930s Provo, Utah. I've still not tried my hand at fiction.

p.s. Although I now own the domain (at regular price, $6 a year) and use it as a repository for essay resources and an anthology of classical essays, when I first tried to register quotidiana.com, it was already owned by a cybersquatter who wanted to sell it to me for $2,500. The handy domain registrar's name-suggester gave me the following alternatives to consider:

> everydaya.com, mundanea.com, routinea.com,
> unremarkablea.com, workadaya.com, ordinarya.
> com, averagea.com, commona.com, mediocrea.com,
> simplea.com, so-soa.com, tolerablea.com, faira.com,
> passablea.com, commonplacea.com, indifferenta.com,
> nondescripta.com, middlinga.com, moderatea.com,
> reasonablea.com, usuala.com, runofthemilla.com

NOTES

1. Speaking of words one wishes for, both Yiddish and French have terms for the witty retort one thinks of only too late, after the heat of verbal battle, when one is on the stairs, on the way out. English, that great amalgamator, must simply borrow these right-on phrases.

Laughter

What is writing other than drawing two letters and
laughing?

MARCEL BÉNABOU *Why I Have Not Written Any of My Books*

As I write — not specifically *now* but generally *in these days* — my
two-and-a-half-month-old daughter is just beginning to laugh,
and I am sharing in her joy, or, if it is not joy that she feels, still
I feel the joy of her laugh. Infants can smile soon after they're
born; some pediatricians say that those fleeting moments are
due to gasses or facial stretches or random chance, and don't
be fooled into thinking she's *really* smiling. I don't know about
that. I don't imagine anybody can say for sure. But now she is
laughing, and I am sure.

She does not laugh only when we laugh; she is not only
mimicking. And it is not because she is ticklish; I have tried
that and it doesn't work. As far as I can tell, she is delighted
by the world. She sees a funny face, sees her brother in a giant
witch's hat, sees me with my glasses on upside down, sees
her mother dancing to the funky music of a commercial, and
she laughs.

I have loved her since she was born — since before she was
born, when she was only a concept to me, an idea — and yet
I do not feel I knew her until now. Her laughter has become

a common ground for us, a realization that the world is an interesting, silly place.

> To laugh, if but for an instant only, has never been granted to man before the fortieth day from his birth, and then it is looked upon as a miracle of precocity.
>
> PLINY THE ELDER *The Natural History*

Which puts her out of "miracle of precocity" range but still within respectable limits. Jupiter, it is said, was born laughing and didn't stop for seven days. According to Barry Sanders, according to Theodore Hopfner, according to a third-century BC Egyptian papyrus, "When [God] burst out laughing there was light. . . . When he burst out laughing the second time the waters were born; at the seventh burst of laughter the soul was born." Man as the height of God's laughter: that might explain a lot of things.

Laugh and the world laughs with you; he who laughs last laughs best; die laughing; laugh your head off; be the laughingstock of; laugh all the way to the bank (the word itself, *laugh*, begins to look ridiculous — misspelled, unintelligible, strangely pronounced); laughter is the best medicine; laugh up your sleeve.

I have tried to be thorough, even having discovered this last one, laugh up your sleeve, which I haven't heard before and which derives from Renaissance times when sleeves were voluminous and available for storage and hiding laughs, but there must certainly be more. Add your own laugh aphorism (laughorism?) in the space provided. Use the fly pages if necessary.

_____

_____

_____

_____

Max Beerbohm, in his essay on this theme, wonders that "of all the countless folk who have lived before our time on this planet not one is known in history or in legend as having died of laughter." But Beerbohm is wrong. Edward Bulwer Lytton's *The Lost Tales of Miletus* speaks of Calchas, a soothsayer who was told by a beggar that he would never drink of the fruit of his vineyard. Moreover, the beggar promised that if his prophecy did not come true, he would be Calchas's slave. Later, when the grapes were harvested and the wine made, Calchas celebrated by laughing so hard at the beggar's folly that he died before he took a sip. More recently, the Joker kills people in Gotham City by laughter, but maybe that's different. He is, after all, inducing the effect artificially, with Smilex gas.

Laughing gas, nitrous oxide, named because of its effect on those who inhale it (disorientation, euphoria, numbness, loss of motor coordination, dizziness, loss of consciousness; I'm not sure who laughs more, a patient anesthetized by the gas or the doctor who administers it), has been used since its discovery in the 1700s as a general anesthetic. Joseph Priestley, who also discovered oxygen and carbon dioxide, called nitrous oxide "an air five or six times as good as common air." The gas is still used to anesthetize dental patients and as a propellant in whipped cream cans. Recent research has linked laughing gas (in high dosages) to birth defects, nerve damage, and permanent organ damage, especially brain damage. As an interesting side note, the 1993 World Trade Center and Oklahoma City bombings involved detonation of laughing gas (a by-product of ammonium nitrate fertilizer), which decomposes explosively into nitrogen and oxygen at high temperatures.

Laughter is like any word: if you say it enough, it begins to sound strange and wondrous. Listen to the sound as it separates from meaning; hear its similarities to other words, its complete uniqueness; feel your tongue pull away from the back of your front teeth, your bottom lip bitten slightly as the air escapes out the sides of your mouth, a quick strike of the tongue, like spitting, cut the air somewhere back of the mouth, in the throat, almost like a vowel, a sound foreigners have difficulty making. It is enough, sometimes, if you say it fast enough long enough, to make you laugh. And if you say it repeatedly with the right rhythm beginning with a quick *da-da* and saying an additional *taf-taf* every third word, you can pick out the *William Tell* overture and call to mind the Lone Ranger, whose faithful Indian friend Tonto's name translates in Spanish to "Fool," which may cause you yet another laugh. Kimosabe, Tonto's name for his masked friend, is of dubious origin, but I have heard it explained as deriving from "Friend" in Potawatomi, "Dancing Frog" in Navajo, and "Who Knows Him" in Portuguese.

> Better of laughter than of tears to write
> For laughter is indeed to man unique.
>
> FRANÇOIS RABELAIS *Gargantua*

This is debatable — the second part that is. The hyena, coarsehaired scavenger of Africa's savannah, is well known as a laugher because of its high, annoying — what-is-it, a bark? a whimper? Monkeys scream out laughter-like sounds in the grasses and the trees of Africa, Asia, and South America. The "laughing jackass," a midsized kingfisher bird native to Australia, makes a loud call that sounds similar to raucous laughter and which tormented early European explorers of that continent. You can hear its laughing call today in an inordinate number of jungle movies, which typically do not take place in Australia. Nowadays the bird prefers to be called by the more politically correct "kookaburra." An old nursery rhyme goes:

Kookaburra sits in the old gum tree.
Merry, merry king of the bush is he.
Laugh, Kookaburra! Laugh, Kookaburra!
Gay your life must be.

This, of course, allows a broad definition of laughter based not on humor but on the sound, the convulsion, the jiggling and giggling. But somebody sometime thought the sound alone was enough to qualify as laughter; thus we learn of the laughing frog (*Rana ridibunda*, which is edible, *ridibunda* meaning  "laughing" in Latin), laughing bird (*Gecinus viridis*, the green woodpecker), the laughing crow or laughing thrush (names used for many Asiatic birds of the genus *Garrulax*), the laughing dove (*Stigmatopelia senegalensis*, the African dove), the laughing goose (*Anser albifrons*, the white-fronted goose), the laughing gull (*Larus atricilla*), the laughing falcon (*Herpetotheres cachinnans*), the laughing owl (*Sceloglaux albifacies*). And it's not only animals that can laugh; in poetry brooks, fires, winds, valleys, fields, wine, seas, plateaus all can laugh as well.

Democritus (460–357 BC) is known as the Laughing Philosopher either because of his cheery disposition and embrace of hedonism or because he laughed at humanity's folly and vanity. He is paired with Heraclitus, the Weeping Philosopher, whose more compassionate response to the same plight of man earned him his nickname.

> Democritus, dear droll, revisit earth,
> And with our follies glut thy heightened mirth.
>
> MATTHEW PRIOR "Democritus and Heraclitus"

Democritus is also known as a proponent (if not originator) of atomic theory. He proposed that matter was not infinitely divisible, that there existed a basic unit of matter, the atom, which was indivisible. Which may bring you to laughter when you consider that even if Democritus was right, we have bungled his theory by giving the name *atom* to that which *can* be further broken down into protons, neutrons, and electrons, which in turn consist of quarks, which name comes not exactly from science but from *Finnegans Wake* because Murray Gell-Mann, proponent and originator of quark theory, so enjoyed that book, or at least the line from the book that goes, "Three quarks for Muster Mark!"

Democritus's influence inspired Robert Burton, author of *The Anatomy of Melancholy*, to give himself the nickname Democritus Junior, because he, too, liked to laugh at the foolishness of mankind. He also liked to make mankind laugh. In his voluminous study of the disease of melancholy (published originally without naming its author until the epilogue), he lists among myriad remedies for the sickness, "Help from Friends by Counsel, Comfort, fair and foul Means, witty Devices, Satisfaction, Musick, Mirth and merry company." In that section he writes that "the Lacedæmonians . . . did sacrifice to the God of Laughter, after their wars especially, and in times of peace . . . because laughter and merriment was to season their labours and modester life. Laughter is the eternal pleasure of gods and men."

Although French words, introduced by England's Norman conquerors centuries ago, transmogrified into a large part of what we now speak as English, many of our elemental, homely words come to us from Old English. *Laughter*, that basic human emotion, is one of them. Somehow this is comforting, as if the perseverance of the word, its steadfastness against the influence of the French *rire*, were transferred to me when I say it.

Yet the word has not remained unchanged. In Old English, the velar fricative, the end sound in a Scottish *loch*, a sound we no longer have in our language, was spelled with an *h*. The Old English root word for laughter is *hleahtor* (or a variation on this), related to words in Old High German and Old Norse, and thought to be imitative, or onomatopoetic in its origin. In Middle English, the spelling of this sound became *gh*. In Early Modern English, competing dialects south of the Humber River caused the *gh* velar fricative sound either to be dropped (plough, though, high) or to be pronounced as an *f*, as in cough, rough, enough, laugh, etc. Linguists postulate that the *f* sound was simply a fallout from a mixing of several dialects. To note the illogic of the change, consider the last name Laughlin, often pronounced *lock-lin*, an approximation of the lost sound, though it contains the word *laugh*.

Though it has not been seen since the mid-nineteenth century, *laughter* has also meant the whole number of eggs laid by a fowl before she is ready to sit. The etymology of this *laughter*, as you might imagine, is different from the one we use today, though one can't help noticing that a trace of *laugh*'s cognates and forebears leads to Proto-Germanic *HlaHjanan*, a cognate with the Greek *klossein*, which means "cluck," as in a chicken.

One of the oldest jokes in the book, one that has never made me laugh (first because I was too young to "get it," then later because it is terribly unfunny), is

"Why did the chicken cross the road?"
"To get to the other side."

And no variation of Chinese newspapers or roosters or beer has ever been able to make me laugh. This, from the point of view of the person telling such a bad joke, is sometimes called "laying an egg."

If I were living when an onomatopoetic word for laughter was being sought, it might be called something like *heah*, with a sharp, pneumatic hiss at the beginning. If we were looking for an imitative name for my friend Anthony's laughter, we'd call it something like *aish aish aish* (kind of annoying, but infectious). There are laughs that are squeals, laughs that are brays, laughs that are vibrato staccato clucks and clicks and snorts. It's no wonder we ascribe laughter to animals. Our own laughter so often mimics animal sounds, which can often mean that laughter feeds itself because, you have to admit, making animal sounds involuntarily is funny all by itself.

In English, laughter as dialogue is most often portrayed as something like "ha ha ha." There are exceptions; for instance, Santa Claus's laugh is "ho ho ho." This is also the laugh of the Green Giant (of canned and frozen vegetable fame). Little people with high voices laugh "hee hee hee," sometimes beginning with a "tee." Connivers or old men or half-laughers do it "heh heh heh." In Spanish, the laugh is represented the same way. Though they are spelled differently, laughs like "ja ja ja," "jo jo jo," "ji ji ji," and "je je je" all sound the same as do our laughs in English. The same holds true for laughs in Romanian, French, Japanese, and Chinese, and I'd be willing to bet it's the same in most other languages, too: always a vowel sound introduced by an *h*, the sound closest to breathing, as if laughter were as basic as respiration.

A partial list of partial synonyms for laughter: cackle, chuckle, chortle, giggle, guffaw, snicker, snigger, titter, twitter. It is worth noting that at least two of the preceding words share syllables with profanity. That, of itself, often causes laughter among children. Had somebody, when I was younger, used the word *titter*, I can guarantee I would have tittered.

I have often heard the questionably accurate legend that the Eskimo language includes dozens or hundreds of words for different kinds of snow, the lesson being that we invent words for the things we experience, the things we need to talk about. I consider it a good sign that we have so many words for laughter.

Many things become laughable only in hindsight, after the emotion of the situation is placated and everything has turned out fine and we can reflect on our good fortune or our dumb luck. Such are my son's many trips to the emergency room for foreign objects in his nose: partially chewed raisins, foam rubber, paper, the tip of a rubber snake's tail. First were the raisins, which happened during my watch when I gave him chocolate-covered ones and left him alone. He sucked off all the chocolate, and — I can only imagine the rest — must have decided to store the unwanted raisins someplace out of the way. My mother has been telling me for as long as I can remember about the raisins I stuck up my nose when I was about my son's same age. To see the genetic code replicate such a banal act is irony at its noblest. But I could not see it as I was struggling with my son under the strong light of the bathroom sink as he tried to break free of my hold as I tried to pull the desiccated masticated grapes from his nostril. We ended up in the hospital then, as did my mother with me twenty-six years earlier, and returned the next day for a visit with the ear, nose, and throat specialist, who has since then become a sort of confidant, and whose staff laughs each time we return. "See," I once overheard a nurse telling her coworker when she saw my son, "I told you it'd be him."

Laughter can unite and comfort because in it people share understanding and happiness. In times of difficulty and sadness, despite Henri Bergson's assertion that laughter and emotion are foes, laughter is often an important healer. It can lighten a heavy burden; it can change the flavor of tears. When our cat died after nineteen years with us, my family was stricken with grief. The cat had been put to sleep at the veterinarian's office, and my brothers drove to pick him up so we could bury him in our backyard. The veterinarian had stuffed the corpse in a thin plastic bag inside a Styrofoam cooler, which was set on the deck as my brothers dug a hole near the woods, one of the cat's favorite haunts, where he had often hunted rabbits and birds and snakes. When the hole was almost finished, my mother and father came carrying the cooler, anxious to finish the burial before it got too dark. Everyone was crying silently, averting eyes and speaking in whispers. Because of the hushed silence, when the diggers took a short rest, my father assumed that the hole was finished and reached into the cooler and removed the bag. But the hole was still too shallow, and as my father made to deposit the cat's body, my brother realized what was going on, calculated instantaneously, and shouted, "Wait! Don't let the cat out of the bag!"

Laughter often breaks down social barriers, draws the curious gaze of the terminally aloof, perturbs the cool imperturbability and silence and feigned disinterest of strangers and passersby and commuters brought together only by their need for transportation. It sometimes allows, for a brief moment only, perhaps, a kind of communion. If Bergson's laughter requires that one feel oneself part of a group, then laughter often forms its own ephemeral groups, united solely for the purpose of laughing, for a moment, before disbanding.

On a train from New York City to New Jersey, late afternoon, Fourth of July, soaring heat, bodies tired from walking: my son can't sit still. He can never sit still, but he is extra-antsy because of the heat, the enclosed space, the challenge of entertaining such a large crowd, who knows? The six of us — me, my wife, my son, my daughter, my father, my sister — have flipped the seatback of one three-seater and are facing one another on two benches as Pato, two-and-a-half, jumps from one bench to the other, heedless, careless of who he kicks or who will catch him. We catch him. He jumps up, hanging from the overhead storage racks until his arms give, and I catch him. He clambers on the seatback, throws his grandfather's hat, drops his crackers, says hello to the man and woman sitting behind us.

I pull him back down, whisper in his ear, plead with him to be still as he wriggles and twists.

He laughs, thinking I am trying to tickle him.

The woman behind ducks to where he can't see her. He steps on my leg to peer over the edge of the seat. She jumps up and whispers, "Boo!"

He falls limp to the seat below, convulsing with laughter.

She does it again. He does it again. She does it again. He does it again. Laughter.

His sister, five months now and well practiced in laughter, stares intently at her brother. Her eyes radiate something I want to call admiration. Each time he falls to the seat beside her, she too laughs heartily, uncontrollably.

By now, passengers in front of us are turning around, not only to watch but to laugh. The woman behind us laughs as she peers around the side of our seat, as she varies her timing and sayings, making animal sounds and creaks. Pato roars like a dinosaur and jumps up and down, hiding and seeking and laughing. Everyone in my family is laughing. My daughter now laughs when Pato falls, when he gets up, when he begins to climb. Her laughter is bright and clear and pure and unselfconscious, and I understand why a cool mountain brook might be said to laugh.

People behind us are sitting up tall in their seats to see the commotion. Some are standing, watching the tireless boy, and asking to see the beautiful little girl who is laughing. They laugh with him as they are entertained by his antics. They laugh with her as they are infected by her wonder. "Is that her?" someone asks. "What a beautiful girl," says another. Across the aisle a teenage girl makes faces and laughs. "Quack quack," says the woman behind.

Pato (whose full name is Patrick, whose mother, who speaks Spanish, nicknamed him Patito — "Little Pat" — to distinguish him from me and my father and grandfather, who then shortened the name to Pato) means, in Spanish, "duck."

> And God said unto Abraham, As for Sarai thy wife, . . . I will bless her, and give thee a son also of her: yea, I will bless her, and she shall be a mother of nations; kings of people shall be of her. Then Abraham fell upon his face, and laughed.
>
> Genesis 17:15–17

In a Bible whose references to laughter mostly point to it as negative — laughing to scorn, the devil laughing — the story of Abraham's reaction to God's news is full of good laughs. I enjoy this passage of scripture, and the one immediately following where Sarah (formerly known as Sarai) also laughs at the prospect of bearing a child at her age (ninety, according to the record), as much as any. I think it is because here God is so accessible, speaking to Abraham, straight-faced, telling him that he will have to put off his retirement plans to raise a child. The cause for laughter is the impossibility of the miracle, the weight of the responsibility if it's true, the awakening to

God's ironic sense of humor, his trials, his special kind of love. It's not easy being chosen, Abraham is beginning to see, and though we know there must have been a glitch somewhere in the translation, we can't help noticing the pratfall: we imagine a dumbstruck Abraham, mouth agape, hair turned just a shade whiter, stumbling and falling as he reels from the news and falls upon his face. That the God-chosen name *Isaac* means "he laugheth" (not so bad when you compare it with the name God chose for Isaiah's son, *Maher-shalal-hash-baz*, which means "the spoil cometh speedily, the prey hasteneth") only heightens the comic effect.

What is this strange relationship between laughter and misfortune? Where is the border between laughter and pity or worry? When a man trips and falls (Bergson's first example of a laughable event), is it always funny? Is it only funny if he is not hurt? When I was younger, ABC introduced their sports programs with a montage of different athletic events and a narrator highlighting the action with general commentary about "The thrill of victory . . . and the agony of defeat." With this line the television showed a ski jumper precariously off-balance on his way down the jump; then he falls and flops like a rag doll as he careens over the edge. I always laughed at that, but I wondered if I should. My father has since told me, without citing his sources, "That guy really got hurt," and I feel almost guilty. What is it then? Disequilibrium? Strange poses? A sigh of relief that it happened to someone else?

At age twelve I am riding on some dirt mounds in a new development of houses near where we live. I'm on a Frankenstein bike that my friend John and I made from salvaged parts.

It's got springs under the vinyl seat and curvy touring-bike handlebars with white hard plastic grips. I'm standing on the pedals, pumping hard to get up an especially steep mound, my thighs burning, arms taut, pulling back, and all of a sudden the grips come flying off the handlebars, simultaneously (I couldn't believe it either), and I'm on my back in the dirt, legs tangled, bike on top of me, two white plastic grips still firmly in my grasp.

We laugh at, with, about clowns, jokes, funny faces, children, ourselves, contortions, misfortunes, wordplay, irony, other laughs, others' joy, good fortune, madness, sickness, health, debilitation, recovery, things we can't change, things we can change, sports, games, circuses, animals, drunkenness, sobriety, sex, celibacy, errors, equivocations, mistakes, blunders, bloopers, boners, double meanings.

With laughter, you often "had to be there." Sometimes even if you weren't there you laugh, but the effect wears off with repeated tellings so that, once again, "you had to be there." I think this points to the difficulty of conveying real experience with language, to the weakness of imitation, as well as to the disparate range of our senses of humor. It means that laughter is often contagious, often set by a mood more than the joke itself or the situation, that experience is never cut off from the sum of prior and concurrent experiences.

From my youth, the funniest in my father's repertoire of childhood stories was this: one day my grandfather bought some fruit trees to plant in the backyard. Among them was a pear tree, which he thought would soon bear fruit. But the pear tree was barren. In the first year, nothing. Likewise the second and the third. The family eventually gave up hope for fruit from the tree; at the same time they had grown rather fond of it. One afternoon my father, his father, and his brothers were tossing the football around in the backyard. Tom goes long for a pass, back to the corner with the pear tree, and when he misses the ball, he falls down flat on his back laughing uncontrollably and pointing to the branches. Everybody runs to him, curious to know why he's laughing. When they ask him what's up, he replies breathlessly, in between convulsions of laughter, "There's an apple on the pear tree!"

The folk wisdom that laughter is the best medicine seems so ingrained in our culture that we believe it in spite of our science worship. We needn't even see extreme examples of laughter-cured ulcers or cancers to know that a positive attitude can work wonders. We have seen it in our own lives.

> Laughter is a form of internal jogging. It moves your internal organs around. It enhances respiration. It is an igniter of great expectations.
>
> NORMAN COUSINS *Head First*

Yet extreme cases do occur. In 1964 the late Norman Cousins, then editor of the *Saturday Review*, was stricken with ankylosing spondylitis, a severe connective tissue disease (in the family of arthritis and rheumatism). Upset with inconsiderate hospital staff, unsanitary conditions, poor nutrition, and a generally depressing hospital environment, he sought ways to help his body heal itself. He researched heavily into the possible causes and cures for his disease, reduced the amount of pain medication he would accept, increased his vitamin C intake, and (this was before the day of the VCR) got a projector and films of *Candid Camera* and several Marx Brothers movies. He also read from several humor anthologies. Soon, with massive vitamin C and laughter, he was out of the hospital and off drugs entirely. The effects of his disease receded rapidly. Eventually, he recovered almost fully, was able to go back to work, and could go about his daily life without pain (he says he could even play Bach's Toccata and Fugue in D Minor, though a little more slowly than before). Although his method of recovery is debated as anything from miracle to placebo, he lived another quarter century, until age seventy-five.

When you laugh, your body moves, your mouth forms a smile, your eyes squint, your nose wriggles. You may throw your head back, shake your head, bite your lower lip, get soda up your nose, close your eyes completely, start to tear, sniffle. Laughing feels good, mostly, and even uncontrollable, painful laughter, where your gut contorts and you can't breathe, serves as a sort of anaerobic exercise. Usually accompanied by happiness, laughter causes an increase in happiness itself. It can even take you out of the doldrums and into — what's the opposite of doldrums? — a hurricane of delight. Medical studies have shown that laughter increases the immune system's activity and decreases stress-producing hormones while increasing good hormones such as endorphins. Cancer and heart patients at Loma Linda University's medical center are treated with episodes of *I Love Lucy* and *The Honeymooners* along with their regular treatments. Laughter has been known to increase levels of disease-fighting T cells, the very cells killed off by AIDS. According to the experts, even fake laughter can sometimes produce these beneficial effects.

> Among those whom I like or admire, I can find no common denominator, but among those whom I love, I can; all of them make me laugh.
>
> W. H. AUDEN *The Dyer's Hand*

That laughter is sweetest which is unexpected, which is inherent in its situation, which takes one unawares. "To that laughter," says Max Beerbohm, "nothing is more propitious than an occasion that demands gravity. To have good reason for not laughing is one of the surest aids." In church, then, in a foreign land, in a foreign language, one might reach such heights of laughter as to lose entirely any semblance of reverence.

In memory, it is a hot Sunday morning in the Carrasco neighborhood of Montevideo, Uruguay. I am one of two gringos among nearly a hundred Uruguayans, both of us missionaries nearing the end of two years of service. The chapel is filled with families in summer dresses and breezy shirts for a sacrament meeting, the Mormon equivalent of a Mass. After a solemn hymn, a member of the congregation approaches the podium to say an opening prayer. "Our kind and gracious Heavenly Father," he begins, and I bow my head, close my eyes, try to keep my mind from wandering as I listen to his prayer. Slowly I become aware of a muffled, tinny music in the air, something like the overflow from too-loud headphones. Appalled at the insolence, the sacrilege of playing a Walkman in the chapel during the meeting, I open my eyes and slyly look around me to find the blasphemer. All other heads are bowed, and none with headphones. I again close my eyes and try to focus, but by now the music is clearer. I try to focus on the words of the prayer, but I am awash in "She's an Easy Lover," by Phil Collins and Phillip Bailey. "She's like no other; before you know it you'll be on your knees." Bailey's falsetto is almost grating, and with another quick peek (my sonolocation system somehow tied to my eyes), I realize that the speakers in the chapel ceiling are channeling the music along with the prayer.

I slide down the bench away from my companion, Elder Lawrence, so as not to laugh. The missionary persona is serious, businesslike (after all, we're teaching the eternal truths: where we came from, why we're here, where we're going), and we often have trouble with it. Lawrence is the kind of guy who can make you laugh just by raising his eyebrows to let you know he's seen what you've seen, and several times before we've lost it during serious religious discussions. This opening prayer is one of the longest I've ever heard, and my mind is slowly breaking down its resistance to laughter. I am nearly hanging over the edge of the bench, bent over in airplane-emergency-landing position, biting my tongue, when I feel the pew start to rumble and shake with Lawrence's silent convulsions. With that the dam of my resolve bursts, and so does Lawrence's, and no amount of turning away, thinking of other things, biting tongues and holding noses shut can stop the laughter. The tears roll down my face, the silent chuckles break through stifles into snorts and clicks, and finally the prayer ends. As the members of the congregation lift their inclined heads and open their eyes, every neck is craned toward us, on every face an expression of confusion and dismay.

> Only the emotion of love takes higher rank than the emotion of laughter.
>
> MAX BEERBOHM "Laughter"

As I write — *now*, in this moment — I can hear my daughter's muted laughter behind me. She is lying in bed, sucking on her whole hand, eyes bright with the morning sun through the window, and she is laughing. It is not clear to me what she is laughing about, but that laughter without motive is beautiful. I listen closely, watching her, and I laugh out loud.

Remember Death

Let us disarm him of his novelty and strangeness, let us converse and be familiar with him, and have nothing so frequent in our thoughts as death. Upon all occasions represent him to our imagination in his every shape; at the stumbling of a horse, at the falling of a tile, at the least prick with a pin. . . . Let us evermore, amidst our jollity and feasting, set the remembrance of our frail condition before our eyes, never suffering ourselves to be so far transported with our delights, but that we have some intervals of reflecting upon, and considering how many several ways this jollity of ours tends to death, and with how many dangers it threatens it.

Where death waits for us is uncertain; let us look for him everywhere. The premeditation of death is the premeditation of liberty.

MONTAIGNE "That to Philosophize Is to Learn to Die"

MR. LAMB, RUSH, VOCABULARY

My eleventh-grade language arts teacher, Mr. Lamb, was a Deadhead (former or ongoing, I do not know, nor could I divine the depth of his deadication), so he encouraged my vocal annotations beside many of our class vocabulary words. "Rush word!" I would call out (in my more exclamatory days) when we happened across *panacea* or *somnolent* or *unobtrusive* or, it seems, hundreds of others that I had learned through listening —

If I may briefly break stride, I must admit my consternation to live in a world where my habitual mentions of Rush inevitably bring the question "Rush Limbaugh?" Would that I could declare, once and for all, a resounding *no*. I haven't the stomach (nor the addled brain) for the man. When I say Rush, it is Rush, the band from Canada that so colored my adolescence as to leave me utterly, shall we say, influenced. The band themselves are not unaware (a trait I grew to admire in their music as I grew older — their *awareness*: of self, of the world) of the problematic homonymic commentator, as evidenced by their tongue-in-cheek instrumental song on 1996's *Test for Echo*, "Limbo." One must imagine it announced by a DJ — an unlikely scenario given that their radio reign ended in the 1980s, and, even now, when a more recent song makes a play list, it is close to the release date of a new album and it is "the single." In any case, what I was aiming for before my sentence got away from me was the band-cum-song: "Rush 'Limbo.'"

To grow up in Whippany, New Jersey, in the 1980s was to be a Rush fan. Everybody I knew liked Rush: for their adolescent sci-fi–themed songs, for their heaviness (musical *and* intellectual), for their complex arrangements and time signatures. But my first contact with Rush came through an outsider, a friend from Maryland.

Here's the scene: "A hot and windy August afternoon has the trees in constant motion." I am ten and impressionable and excited and in the way-back of my mother's tan Volare station wagon with my older, wiser friend Robert. My mother is driving, I assume, and we are about to pull out of the driveway, or have just pulled in, we're idling, waiting for the miracle that is about to take place. In memory the leaves on the birch tree in my front yard move, but we never move. Robert has a Walkman and a mix tape. He places the headphones on my ears, raises an eyebrow, and, I swear, his eyes glint. He says, "Listen to this," presses play, and my head is filled with the spacey keyboard explosion, the quick drumbeat, the echoey androgynous high-pitched voice, like a witch:

A modern-day warrior
Mean, mean stride
Today's Tom Sawyer
Mean, mean pride.

Dun dun da-dunhhh!

I was hooked, and I'm convinced that it wasn't predispositionary, because just after "Tom Sawyer" on the tape was UB40's version of Neil Diamond's "Red, Red Wine," which Robert played over and over, and which I did not like. (It took until I was married to a member of the Columbia House CD club with extra free CDs to get before I even half-owned a copy of *The Very Best of UB40*, which consists of "Red, Red Wine," a cover of Sonny and Cher's "I Got You Babe" sung with Chrissie Hynde, a cover of the Doors' "Light My Fire," a cover of Elvis's "Can't Help Falling in Love," and the ironically titled "Sing Our Own Song." There are other songs on the album, but I'd never heard them before.) Rush, on the other hand, became the soundtrack to my life, their songs' expressions and allusions my gateway to a new world, to literature we didn't read in school, to movies and art and science: beyond Mark Twain, whom we've covered already, there was Ayn Rand, John Dos Passos, Ernest Hemingway, William Faulkner, William Shakespeare, Sherwood Anderson, Frank Capra, Orson Welles, Mel Brooks, Samuel Taylor Coleridge, John Barth, Benoit Mandelbrot, J. R. R. Tolkien, Miguel de Cervantes,

John Steinbeck, Paul Gauguin, Stanley Kubrick, Edward Hicks, Sir Francis Beaufort, Cassius Marcellus Coolidge, Leonardo da Vinci, Peter Ilyich Tchaikovsky, Rod Serling, the list goes on and on . . .

> The records are bought by people when they hit puberty, when it becomes important to us to attach to ideas . . . to discover how we think.
>
> ROGER WATERS "Roger Waters Breathes Easier"

Rush became my sounding board, my trolling net, my filter for apprehending the world.

That same year I took Mr. Lamb's language arts class, the year my best friend, Vin, and I transformed Hester Prynne into a comic-book superhero (*The Ubiquitous Scarlet Auspex,* complete with large-red-A-on-chest uniform) for our final class "paper," I gave my Academic Decathlon "prepared speech" on Rush. I didn't want to do any work preparing, so I spoke about something I knew intimately, which explains my poor evaluation in that category (though I won in science, or took third, and possibly in some other category as well, and scored higher, overall, in ten events, than anyone else on my high school team, which was pretty good, considering there were several sophomore girls there who seemed to know everything and to care desperately about the competition — studying for weeks beforehand, practicing their speeches, reviewing old SATS — while I and my cronies, Mark and Vin, took the attitude that you could ask us to go to the thing, but we weren't going to waste any energy on it). These girls were friends of ours from our classes (where we were a year ahead, in math, for instance, they were two years ahead) and the track team, though we once, tinged with jealousy, I think, determined that what they were really good at was rote, astonishing memorization, taking tests.

Just as birds sometimes go in quest of grain, and carry it in their beak without tasting it to give a beakful to their little ones, so our pedants go pillaging knowledge in books and lodge it only on the end of their lips, in order merely to disgorge it and scatter it to the winds.

MONTAIGNE "Of Pedantry"

Vin was the one who said that if you gave them a problem slightly different from the ones in the book, they'd be lost. I can't remember if he had done the experiment or if he was just imagining it. So while most of the kids in our calculus class were designing their extra-credit bulletin boards with exact replicas of diagrams and formulas from the text, Vin and I ripped all previous bulletin boards to shreds, and inspired all future ones, with our parabolical, diabolical Joker device, which filled slowly with water to demonstrate a time-dependent change in volume of a three-dimensional cone, and to kill Batman and Robin, who were tightly bound and struggling (as much as construction paper can be made to struggle) to escape, with the help of quick-calculating calculus students, within the allotted time.

BRENDA MILLER, *MEMENTO MORI*, ROLL THE BONES

But we are not really talking about death, you will have noticed, let alone remembering it, unless we are willing to stretch to the unintentional (though factual) Grateful Dead reference with which we started the essay, and the recent allusion to imminent death on the bulletin board. But let us get to the genesis of this essay, where Rush and vocabulary words will tie in (and perhaps pedantry as well).

I went to the University of Utah on October 14, 2004, to hear a reading by poet Albert Goldbarth and essayist Brenda Miller. It was great, spectacular, inspirational, whathaveyou, but really I was fatigued from a day filled with empty tasks and water-treading, so that I filtered the readers' words like a seine filters plankton. I grasped nothing. Miller read an essay about a lover, told in the second person, then an essay about an artist in post-9/11 New York City lithographing airplanes in bright colors from all angles, hanging the prints to dry on clotheslines crisscrossing her studio. I was left with only gists, on my way to nothing more than superficial osmosis, when, like an invocation, Miller pronounced the words that inspired this essay: *memento mori*. For me, they came free, detached from context, connecting only to the meaning I already held within my head.

I *knew* "*memento mori.*" I perked up, though not to listen to Miller's essay. Instead, I jotted down on the backside of a June 21, 2004, handwritten note from Vin (which I found folded up in my back pocket) the whirling associations now wriggling in my net, surfacing from the depths of my memory:

Roll the Bones . − . . − − . − etc.
"Let the dead bury their dead"
Yes, but he knew he was coming back
Theroux's meditation on more gruesome Christs in
    Latin America
Peter Ho Davies's meditation on calm sports crowds in USA
John Levis unrecognized at reunion where I wasn't there
Memento (movie) Guy Pierce

(Alas, in this essay I will deal only with the first two, having let them drive my thoughts to other, more fertile pastures, and having, in two instances, forgotten completely what I was thinking, how they connect, why I wrote such things down.)

> A crowd of considerations gathers.
> Here I can pay heed only to a few.
>
> WILLIAM GASS *On Being Blue*

Before this handwritten note, which accompanied a nearly two-year-old family portrait ("Kate now looks much older," it said), Vin hadn't written to me for years, aside from brief e-mails, yet I didn't think much of the fact that of all the scrap papers I typically carry in my back pocket — lesson plans, bills, announcements, zero-percent-interest credit card offers — I had only this note, which was on my person several months after I had received it (and probably should have thrown it away) because a student of mine (who happened also to be my neighbor's niece) had handwriting that so reminded me of Vin's that I had to show it to her.

I knew "*memento mori*" because of the 1991–92 Rush *Roll the Bones* tourbook, which included in its inside front cover a cryptic message in skull-and-femur Morse code. I saw Rush a few times on this tour, including near the beginning of the tour at the Palace at Auburn Hills, Michigan (I was attending Notre Dame), on November 13, 1991, along with my hometown friend John Anderson (who was attending Michigan State); I saw them again near the end of the tour, on June 19, 1992, at the Meadowlands, in East Rutherford, New Jersey, again with John Anderson, who was, like me, back home in Whippany for the summer. As soon as I got back to my dorm from the Michigan show, I deciphered the message — "Remember Death" — but I had nothing to connect it to until, a few months later, Neil Peart, Rush's drummer and lyricist, answered in a newsletter a fan's question about the quote (and the *Roll the Bones* album cover, which pictured a boy kicking a skull while shuffling with his hands in his jeans pockets along a broken-down path in front of a wall of dice that became more random and chipped from top to bottom —

> In my childhood, we boys played a game: we would
> watch the gravedigger at work. Sometimes he would
> hand us a skull, with which we would play soccer.
> For us that was the delight which no funereal thought
> came to darken.
>
> E. M. CIORAN All Gall Is Divided)

Said Peart:

The cover art reflects a style of 17th-century Dutch
painting called *vanitas*, in which symbols, such as the
skull (and also candles, books, flowers, playing cards,
etc.), were used to remind the good Netherlanders of
life's brevity, and the ultimate transience of all material
things and sensual pleasures. These paintings sometimes
used a Latin motto: "*memento mori*," which translates as
"remember death."

I had never noticed such paintings, and I didn't go in search of them then (there was no World Wide Web), but I have done so recently. The form may be traced, as Mr. Peart directs, to early seventeenth-century Dutch still-lifes, notably those of Jacques de Gheyn I, II, and III, David Bailly, and Harmen Steenwijck. The most common reminder of death certainly was the skull, though in addition to those items in Peart's list, bubbles, mirrors, candles, clocks, musical instruments, etc. also contributed to the didactic message of such paint-ings: reminders to the Netherlands of the Netherworld. It would seem the scriptural inspiration for this new style of

Dutch painting came from Ecclesiastes: "Vanity of vanities; all is vanity" and "In all thy works be mindful of thy last end and thou wilt never sin."

The earliest *vanitas* work is Jacques de Gheyn the Elder's *Vanitas Still Life*, in which Democritus and Heraclitus, the laughing and weeping philosophers, point their fingers of droll scorn or pity at a scene below consisting of a skull, cut flowers, smoke, Spanish coins, a bubble, and, in the bubble, a wheel of torture, a leper's rattle, a broken glass, a flaming heart. Which is to say that *vanitas* is a hodgepodge, a collection of disparate objects hinting toward a mysterious meaning, relying on interesting and incongruous interconnections and allusions; a *vanitas* is a sort of painted essay.

The biblical invitation "let us eat and drink; for tomorrow we shall die," another *memento mori*, which most readers today see as a heathen's motto, is not unique to, did not originate in the Bible, and thus may have sincerely expressed the belief that the afterlife was no time for even innocuous carnal pursuits (though the resurrected Jesus notably eats some fish and honeycomb). Horace, for example, in his "Cleopatra Ode," declares. "*Nunc est bibendum, nunc pede libero / pulsanda tellus*," which may be translated as: "Now is the time to drink, now the time to dance footloose upon the earth."

The term *footloose* probably derives from sailing — a mainsail's bottom edge (the "foot") could either be stretched by a boom (which one might, in other circumstances, lower) or, at times or on certain vessels, be left unattached; thus the sail was "footloose" — although the poet Joseph Beaumont used the term quite literally (meaning "with unbound feet") in 1648's *Psyche, or Loves Mysterie*, before the term took on the more metaphorical association of "footloose and fancy free." For my generation, though, *Footloose* is the 1984 movie (and accompanying Kenny Loggins song) about dancing: teenagers rebelling against their oppressive, pharisaical parents who have prohibited it. *Footloose* was filmed, in part, at the Roller Mills in Lehi, Utah, where I now live. I am not sure if this qualifies me and my fellow townspeople to claim a connection to Kevin Bacon, but if it does, we are no more than two degrees separated from the man, which is a lot closer than the requisite six to get to any other film actor in Hollywood. (An actor with my name, Patrick Madden, who plays the part of "dancer" in a nine-minute 2004 Russian film called *Friday Night Fever*, has a "Bacon number" of four, according to the Oracle of Bacon at the University of Virginia [oracleofbacon.org].)

JEROME, PAUL THE HERMIT, DÜRER

For Christians, remembering death, or The Death (of Christ), has long been a regular, inescapable practice. Crucifixes and crosses adorn churches and necklaces, relief carvings or stained-glass windows or oil paintings represent the fourteen Stations of the Cross, readings and homilies and preachings remind

and remonish. At Mass on Good Friday when I was growing up, Father John, along with two lectors perched on either side of the altar, read from John's gospel, acted out the reading in parts, and we, too, the congregation, chimed in, playing the part of the crowd. "We have no king but Caesar," we scoffed in unison. "Crucify him! Crucify him!" we remocked. Then he is taken to Golgotha, the place of the skull.

Of course, painted skulls do not suddenly appear in the Netherlands in the seventeenth century. Fourteenth-century woodcuts and engravings of dancing skeletons or skeletons paired with living persons reflect the belief that the dead rose at midnight to dance before wandering off to recruit from among the living. This was the *danse macabre*, artistic response to the Black Death. The skull also appears symbolically in religious paintings and engravings, often alongside the penitent (such as Mary Magdalene) or the hermit. One such hermit, portrayed by Pieter Brueghel the Elder, El Greco, Leonardo da Vinci, Hierony-mous Bosch, Rembrandt, and scores of others, was Saint Jerome (also called Hieronymous), a Doctor of the Church who lived from 340 to 420 and is best known for translating the Bible from Hebrew and Greek into Latin. Although he was born in a Christian home, he was not baptized until he went to Rome (to study Greek and other subjects) at age twenty. Some years later, he traveled to Antioch, where, during an illness, he had a vision that convinced him to leave behind his secular studies and devote his life to religious writings. At this time he also withdrew from public life to perform an ascetic penance in the desert. Upon his return to Antioch, he was ordained a priest; then he returned to Rome, as an advisor to Pope Damasus; then he traveled widely before once again aparting himself to a sanctuary near Bethlehem, where he remained for the last thirty-four years of his life.

Jerome was a prolific writer, contributing not only his translation of the Bible but many exegetical works on the scriptures and theological controversies (including the first Latin commentary on Ecclesiastes based on the original Hebrew), various letters, and historical works, among them the *Life of Saint Paul the Hermit*. Jerome began this project to contro-

vert or supplement the various histories of Saint Anthony, whom many (erroneously) believed to be the first religious hermit. In this book, we learn that Anthony, at age ninety, began to believe that he was the most pious, the most abnegated, the most ascetic fish in the hallowed desert-hermit pond. But God revealed to him in a dream that this was not so. Anthony wanted either proof or absolution, so he did what any of us would have done: he went wandering aimlessly in the desert trying to find this other, more hardcore hermit. Along the way, he ran into a centaur who pointed him in the right direction, and then, before he finally met and embraced and broke bread with Paul (who was, at that time, 113 years old and very near death), he met a satyr, who fed him and asked for Anthony's intercessory prayers. This, cries Anthony, is the final defeat of Satan: even the beasts of Hades recognize the Christ. Jerome assures us that the satyr was real:

> Let no one scruple to believe this incident; its truth is supported by what took place when Constantine was on the throne, a matter of which the whole world was witness. For a man of that kind was brought alive to Alexandria and shewn as a wonderful sight to the people. Afterwards his lifeless body, to prevent its decay through the summer heat, was preserved in salt and brought to Antioch that the Emperor might see it.

Jerome himself inspired legends, too, most notably that he removed a thorn from a lion's paw and this lion was thenceforth his constant companion and sometime pack animal. A similar thing happened to Androcles before Aesop wrote it down in the sixth century BC (the moral of that story — in which Androcles is captured and thrown to the friendly lion as punishment, then is pardoned when he is miraculously saved — is "Gratitude is the sign of noble souls"). It also happened to a mouse, according to an African folktale. Thus appears Jerome's lion lying placidly in the forefront of an engraving by Albrecht Dürer (who painted or engraved Jerome repeatedly) called *Saint Jerome in His Study*. On the shelf to Jerome's right rests the ever-present skull.

I first met Dürer on the back cover of another Rush tourbook, for 1990's *Presto* tour, where his famous *Young Hare* serves as counterpoint to the Fibonaccian rabbits photographed on the front cover. Inside that tourbook, in his customary essay, Neil Peart invokes Stendhal's maxim (which Stendhal attributes to Saint-Real, and which Peart misattributes to either Flaubert or Balzac) that "a novel is a mirror carried along a main road." Henry James prefaced *The Portrait of a Lady* with his vision of fiction as a house, with a million windows, and

> at each of them stands a figure with a pair of eyes, or at least with a field-instrument, insuring to the person making use of it an impression distinct from any other.

But what of essays, unwieldy beasts, double-tongued thens-and-nows, founts of meditations and consternations? George Orwell, topping off his mea culpa "Why I Write," concurs, in a sense, with James: "Good prose is like a windowpane."

Mirrors and windows. Wrote Paul: "For now we see through a glass, darkly; but then face to face: now I know in part; but then shall I know even as also I am known." The now is where I'm at, and, for me, where *it's* at: the hazy partial reflections, partial seeings-through, the knowing in part, the impossibility of knowingitall.

Or perhaps Papa Montaigne, dispensing with the metaphors, may guide:

> These are my . . . true stories, which I find as entertaining
> and as tragic as those that we make up at will in order to
> give pleasure. . . . And if anyone should wish to build up
> an entire and connected body of them, he would need to
> furnish only the connecting links, . . . and by this means
> he could amass a great many true events of all sorts,
> arranging and diversifying them as the beauty of the
> work should require.
>
> "Of Three Good Women"

THOMAS

From Golgotha, side pierced by a spear, Jesus was taken down from the Rood and placed in Joseph of Arimathea's sepulchre, wrapped in linen clothes and anointed with myrrh and aloes bought by Nicodemus, he who had missed the metaphor when Jesus told him to be born again. On Sunday morning he appeared to Mary Magdalene, to Mary the mother of James, and to Cleopas and another disciple on the road to Emmaus, before visiting ten of his apostles. I have always felt a sympathy for, a connection to Thomas, called Didymus, the twin, who was away running errands for the others when the Lord surreptitiously returned to the upper room, declared Peace unto them who cowered and skulked. Thomas, the bold, victim of too many practical jokes at the hands of his apostolic brethren, refuses to believe them, declares defiantly, "Except I shall see in his hands the print of the nails, and put my finger into the print of the nails, and thrust my hand into his side, I will not believe." Who can blame him? Certainly not the ten, who, when confronted with Mary Magdalene's testimony, and that of the travelers to Emmaus, also disbelieved for a brief moment until they heard "Peace be unto you," then saw the marks of the nails. And eight days later, as they still shrank, before the Pentecost, that

> holy day of language, mendingover of the Tower of Babel fiasco,
>
> MICHAEL DANKO "Whistling in the Dark"

before they replaced Judas Iscariot with Matthias, who drew the short straw, whose name may have sired my surname, Madden, from the Irish O'Madadhain (that is if it doesn't mean "little dog" in Gaelic) — eight days later he returns, and Thomas is with them, remembering, putting things together. But Thomas was emphatic, and John remembered and recorded his challenge, whereas the others were together in their collective doubt, so that Thomas became a metaphor: doubting Thomas, patron saint of essayists.

LET THE DEAD BURY THEIR DEAD

Jesus is most famous for his parables about loving one's neighbor and doing good, but every now and then he saddled his hearers with a paradox so lively, so enigmatic, that they, and now we, look the other way. We pretend he never said it. One of these sayings, which has bothered me from the first time I heard it, is "let the dead bury their dead." Jesus has just delivered his greatest hits, the beatitudes, from high on a mountain to a throng of people below. He has just taught his disciples how to pray with the "Our Father." "No man can serve two masters," he instructed. "Consider the lilies of the field," he directed. "Take no thought for the morrow," he challenged. And there are people wanting to hear more, wanting to follow this eloquent dusty man, to *get* what he's saying, to walk the walk like he does. Great multitudes are chasing after him, a leper wants to be healed and with a word he's healed, a centurion — a *centurion* for Pete's sake — has a sick servant, Jesus says he'll be right there, but the guy knows that Jesus can work even long distance, says the words we repeated every Mass — "Lord, I am not worthy to receive you, but only say the word" — which he does, and Matthew checked up on it later, assuring us that "his servant was healed in the selfsame hour." He heals Peter's mother-in-law, casts out devils, fulfilling Esaias's prophecies, and people want to join up. A scribe comes along; Jesus warns him that life with him means sleeping in the dust, relying on the kindnesses of strangers. Then another man comes, hoping not to miss the boat, explaining that he'll be right back, he just has to bury his father. And Jesus will have none of it: "Follow me, and let the dead bury their dead."

Did Thomas remember this saying later, when Jesus, impatient with his apostles' misapprehension of metaphor, risked stoning by returning to Bethany, to comfort Martha, whom he loved, and her sister, Mary, whom he loved, to awaken their brother, Lazarus? ("Our friend Lazarus sleepeth" he had said, "but I go, that I may awake him out of sleep." Then said his disciples, "Lord, if he sleep, he shall do well." Then said Jesus unto them plainly, "Lazarus is dead.") Jesus said, "I am glad for your sakes that I was not there, to the intent ye may believe; nevertheless let us go unto him." Then Thomas, always keen to follow Jesus, calming fears or catching his master in a contradiction, careful not to ascribe his pronoun, leaves us with a useful ambiguity: "Let us also go," he says, "that we may die with him." Let the dead bury their dead, indeed.

Vin's Eagle Scout project, which he completed (with my help) sometime in 1987, was to clean and catalog nineteenth-century veterans' gravestones in the Whippany Burying Yard, which includes stones as early as 1718 (John Richards II — a local schoolmaster whose nine-year-old daughter, Jemima, was kidnapped by Indians in 1704 — donated the land only three months before he himself was buried there). The oldest are squat stones with gothic lettering and graven images of winged cherubs or skeletons across their arched tops. When we saw them, the images seemed incongruous, slightly discomfiting, and we joked that they indicated the final resting place of the interred. Richards's own stone bears a death's-head and the inscription "Here Lyes Ye Body of John Richards, Aged 63 Years." It is made of sandstone but has been encased in granite since 1914. Years after Vin's Eagle project, I worked for a summer mowing grass for the town parks and recreation commission, and each time we mowed that cemetery we found stones knocked over, some falling slowly down a mud embankment into the Whippany River, victims of sudden rains, river swells, a slow, steady erosion.

One Veterans Day, in the Holy Rood cemetery nearby, my father and I, along with Paul Mooney and his father, were to place American flags in the grass atop the tombs of local veterans. My father had a map with the sites marked, and we parked near one grave assembly. Upon exiting the car, I noticed, almost immediately, that the nearest headstone said MADDEN. As I was pointing this out to my father, laughing nervously, I glanced to the side and saw that its next door neighbor was LEPORE, just like our next-door neighbor back at home. We were already thinking spooky thoughts, and this collocation was a message to us. Soon we finished our decorating in that vicinity and moved on to another part of the cemetery. Primed to look for it, we immediately found the MOONEY headstone right next to our car there. Now everyone was in on the game. At our next stop, it was another MADDEN, and after that, a MADDEN and a MOONEY close together. Both of our families were first-generation New Jerseyans. None of the deceased were our relatives. Thinking back, I can believe that we must have paused in places where there were no correlated stones, but memory has stored this perfection: that *everywhere* we stopped we found our names engraved beside us.

Oscar Berliner, quoting his mother, likely from Yiddish (he makes a point of translating into English), in his son Alan Berliner's film *Nobody's Business*:

When you remind yourself of death, you become less certain of living.

"TEMPUS FUGIT," JOHN ANDERSON
Where tombstones inherently remind us of death, timepieces, too, may be apt symbols of mortality, and public clocks often bore the inscriptions *ultima forsan* ("perhaps the last" [hour]) or *vulnerant omnes, ultima necat* ("all wound, the last kills"). Even today, some clocks carry the motto *tempus fugit*, "time flies."

A memory, on Boulevard Road in Cedar Knolls, New Jersey, about which road I have no other distinct memories, but a general feeling of linguistic glee at its redundancy: our older friends gone to college in Colorado and Texas, I find myself alone with John Anderson, whose musical tastes match mine, and who will die surfing at age thirty after we've lost touch. Here, then, he has passed the halfway point of his life. I am only recently understanding the music of Yes, and John, whose namesake Jon Anderson sings for the band, is driving us somewhere after a track meet, playing a song I have never heard.

Its title: "Tempus Fugit." This was the first time I heard the phrase. From osmotic listenings to Franz Biebel's "Ave Maria" and my father's offhand Latin comments, I understand what it means. It is one of those songs whose title tells you what it is, though it does not appear anywhere in the lyrics. John quizzes me. It sounds like Jon Anderson's voice, but, no, he tells me, it's Trevor Horn, the guy from the Buggles. "Video Killed the Radio Star"? I make like I believe him, but check later anyway. What do you know.

I don't know exactly how John died, though there were frantic e-mails from old friends, a copied-and-pasted obituary from San Diego, and rumors of a heart attack, and I wondered how a thirty year-old heart gives out. His mother died a month or so later, and I remembered the last time I had seen his quiet father, when I locked the keys in my car at the post office down the hill, where I had caught up with Mr. Belusko, the postmaster, who told me about his daughter Deanna's dance studies in Europe. I knocked on the Andersons' door, introduced myself as John's old friend, and Mr. Anderson agreed to let me use the phone, though he never really committed to remembering me. "Tempus Fugit" reworks its meaning, becomes a kind of dirge when I check on it, pull it out of its case and give it a listen after so many years:

> If you could see all the roads I have traveled towards
>   some unusable last equilibrium
> Run like an athlete and die like a dead beaten speed-
>   freak.

"YYZ," ALIVE!, 9/11

The "Remember Death" bit was not Rush's only foray into Morse code. Their Grammy-nominated 1981 instrumental "YYZ" begins with Neil Peart's off-beat ride cymbal

−.−− −.−− −−.. (Y-Y-Z, the transmitter code for Toronto's Lester B. Pearson International Airport) setting the time at 10/4. Rush lost the Grammy that year to the Police's "Behind My Camel," a dated, repetitive bit of cacophonous electronica that nobody remembers (though "YYZ" remains an AOR staple to this day). They lost in the same category in 1992, 1994, 2005, 2008, and 2009 to (respectively) "Cliffs of Dover" by Eric Johnson (who opened for them at the Michigan *Roll the Bones* show that John and I saw), "Marooned" by Pink Floyd, "Mrs. O'Leary's Cow" by Brian Wilson, "Once Upon a Time in the West," an Ennio Morricone composition performed by Bruce Springsteen, and "Peaches in Regalia" by Zappa Plays Zappa. "YYZ," the song, according to Peart, "is loosely based on airport-associated images: exotic destinations, painful partings, happy landings."

When I think of airports and airplanes, I sometimes think of the Friday, October 13, 1972, crash in the Andes mountains by a rugby team from Montevideo, Uruguay. I think of their three-month ordeal, their decision to eat the flesh of the dead, their miracle hike out, their rescue. I think of this because a) when I was young, I read the account of their ordeal in Piers Paul Read's book *Alive*, which Vin lent to me (Read has written, too, about the Knights Templar, who were decimated on Friday, October 13, 1307, when King Philip IV of France had thousands arrested, tortured, and then killed; this, it is believed, is the origin of the superstition about Friday the thirteenth as a day of bad luck); b) despite that, I have never seen the Ethan Hawke (Bacon number: 2) film version of the ordeal; c) I have lived in Uruguay for almost four years, all told; d) my wife grew up in Uruguay and was attended, when she was young, by heart doctor Roberto Canessa, one of the sixteen survivors and one of two who hiked to civilization; e) recently an American hiker discovered survivor

Eduardo Strauch's wallet and returned it to him. Said Strauch: "It reminds me of some happy moments we had up there on the mountain, spiritual moments as well as all the suffering and pain we went through." As if he could have said anything else. He cannot escape, and the world will continue to cast brief glances to the South whenever we are reminded of the grotesque and the complex, the no simple answers, the horror of a necessary anthropophagy. I will remember that indirectly, but not too indirectly, my children are alive because one man ate another. *Take, eat; this is my body.*

I also sometimes think of the September 2001 crashes in New York and Washington DC and Pennsylvania of four passenger planes hijacked by terrorists and used as missiles to demolish the Twin Towers and part of the Pentagon. I think of thousands dead and my country's security shattered and a crick in the neck from looking over our shoulders. And this is where we began: with Brenda Miller's essay about her painter friend painting airplanes, hanging them on clotheslines: head-on planes, side-view planes, one plane, two planes, red planes, blue planes.

"NEW YEAR'S EVE," SAINT ANTHONY
AND HIS PORTRAYERS

But now, shall I confess a truth? . . . I begin to count
the probabilities of my duration, and to grudge at the
expenditure of moments and shortest periods, like
miser's farthings. In proportion as the years both lessen
and shorten, I set more count upon their periods, and
would fain lay my ineffectual finger upon the spoke of
the great wheel. I am not content to pass away "like a
weaver's shuttle." Those metaphors solace me not, nor
sweeten the unpalatable draught of mortality. I care not
to be carried with the tide that smoothly bears human

life to eternity; and reluct at the inevitable course of destiny. I am in love with this green earth; the face of town and country; the unspeakable rural solitudes, and the sweet security of streets. I would set up my tabernacle here. I am content to stand still at the age to which I am arrived; I, and my friends: to be no younger, no richer, no handsomer. I do not want to be weaned by age; or drop, like mellow fruit, as they say, into the grave.

CHARLES LAMB "New Year's Eve"

Like Lamb, I cannot imagine not being, cannot imagine being at peace with death, arriving at a point where I await it calmly or eagerly. I read with interest but without comprehension the account of Seneca's death, decreed by his former pupil Nero, whom he had taught despite the conflict between Nero's opulence and elitism and Stoicism's doctrines of simplicity and equality. When Nero's officers demanded Seneca's suicide, refusing him even a moment to set his affairs in order, Seneca willingly complied, according to the dictates of the Stoicism he had preached, offering as an inheritance to his fellows the example of his life. Then,

With a single stroke of the blade, they sliced [his] arms. Seneca, hardened by frugal living, did not bleed easily. He cut the veins of his knees and thighs. But still he did not die. He asked his doctor to dispense some poison Hemlock. He drank it in vain. Finally, he was carried into the baths, where he suffocated in vapor.

TACITUS *Annals*

His calm acceptance, even welcoming of such a gruesome, drawn-out death (as a lamb to the slaughter), bemuses me. The spirit indeed is willing but the flesh is strong. I am better able to comprehend Seneca's earlier words regarding his living on for the sake of his wife —

Sometimes, though occasions importune us to the contrary, we must call back life, even though it be with torment: we must hold the soul fast in our teeth.

"Epistulae ad Lucilium"

— or, from another of his letters to Lucilius, his justification for my including his story, and others', here:

Whatever is well said by another is mine.

I have been taught that there awaits us after death an everlasting peace, an unimaginable reward for the penitent, that the honorable needn't fear, yet there is in me some fear, some longing to stay long, to stick with what I know and love. I am, alas, more cynical than Senecal.

As for Lamb, barely a decade after he published his essay, he contracted erysipelas, a streptococcal disease of the skin, from a cut on his face, which he got when he fell during a walk. Erysipelas begins as a small abrasion, then soon grows and hardens into a fiery-red, shiny rash, sometimes with blisters. Sufferers usually experience fevers and chills, nausea, and muscle and joint pain. The streptococci that cause erysipelas may travel through the blood and damage the sufferer's heart valves and kidneys. Today, erysipelas is treated with penicillin and is rarely fatal. As it was, Lamb missed another New Year's Eve by only a few days, dying on December 27 or 29, 1834. Then, one supposes, he knew, along with Horace, the answer to his question:

> Sun, and sky, and breeze, and solitary walks, and summer holidays, and the greenness of fields, and the delicious juices of meats, and fishes, and society, and the cheerful glass, and candle-light, and fireside conversations, and innocent vanities, and jests, and irony itself — do these things go out with life?
> "New Year's Eve"

That erysipelas is today known as Saint Anthony's Fire is considered by many to be a mistake due to its similarity to ergotism, which is also, or more correctly, known as Saint Anthony's Fire. Doesn't *ergotism* sound like it should mean something like "the arrogance of Descartes and his followers"? But it doesn't. It means a gangrenous or convulsive disease caused by ingested ergots, funguses that grow with rye. In the Middle Ages, ergotism epidemics were common, leaving large swaths of the population mad or dead after driving them to hallucinations and rotting off their extremities. Some scholars believe that ergotism was the cause of the Salem witchcraft trials of 1692, which came about after eight girls who exhibited strange behaviors — including convulsive speech, postures, and gestures — were diagnosed with "bewitching," and started naming names. Ergot, in small doses, is used to stop bleeding after childbirth and to mitigate migraine headaches.

The name Saint Anthony's Fire may derive from the sensation of being burned or from the hallucinations and madness that accompany the searing pain of the disease. Saint Anthony, whom we've met already, was an Egyptian monk who lived from 251 to 356. His parents both died when he was twenty, and he inherited a sizable fortune. At Mass one Sunday, he heard Jesus' counsel to the young rich man — "If thou wilt be perfect, go and sell that thou hast, and give to the poor, and thou shalt have treasure in heaven: and come and follow me" — felt it was directed to him, and did as directed. He spent decades living in isolation on the outskirts of Alexandria, then in a tomb, which he sealed up to avoid contact with admirers, accepting only scant meals and dispensing advice through a small door. Then he moved to an abandoned Roman fort. He was repeatedly tempted by the devil, whose devices included boredom, women, soldiers, and fantastic beasts that beat Anthony and repeatedly left him moribund. Each time he prayed fervently and recovered fully. Despite his desire to remove himself entirely from human intercourse, he eventually decided to "put aside the alienation," ceding to the pleas

of other ascetics who had gathered in huts and caves around his fort. Thus, he organized a group of disciples, the first order of monks. (Though he was not the first monk, he was the first abbot.) He moved again, soon thereafter, to the desert between the Nile and the Red Sea, where he lived in a cave for the last forty-five years of his life, seeing whatever visions and visitors came to him and, infrequently, traveling to nearby cities. In one of his few excursions, Anthony went to Alexandria, seeking a martyr's death. There he comforted Christian prisoners and confronted the angry governor, who commanded him to leave. He lived. Alack.

Flaubert wrote about him. Heironymous Bosch painted him (repeatedly), as did Pieter Brueghel the Elder, or one of his followers, and his son, Jan Brueghel the Elder. So did Cézanne, Goya, Dalí, others. When, in 1512, the monks at Saint Anthony's monastery in Isenheim commissioned an altarpiece for their hospital chapel, Matthias Grünewald (not his contemporary Albrecht Dürer, as was once believed) painted a polyptych with a dark, writhing (as much as paint can be made to writhe), crucified Christ at the center; in one wing the angular *Meeting of Saint Anthony and Saint Paul the Hermit*; and in another, the *Temptation of Saint Anthony*. In this painting, horrible demons and deformed creatures rush forward into and over Anthony, who is literally taken aback, pulled by the hair, about to be trampled, beaten, cut, bled, torn asunder, annihilated. In a moment, in a surge of adrenaline and supplication, Anthony will be saved once more. Behind the embattled Anthony, in the forefront of the fray, almost as grotesque as the attacking monsters, sits a human figure rife with boils, head back

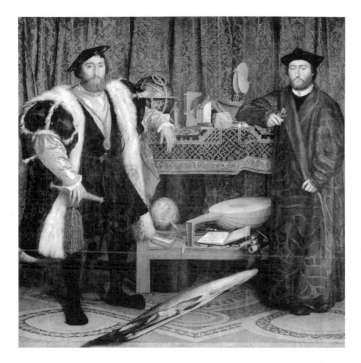

in agony. This is a victim of Saint Anthony's Fire, whom the monks treated in their hospital. That Matthias Grünewald is today known as Matthias Grünewald is considered by many to be a mistake due to an early scholar's misguided research or Grünewald's own designs. Although he is now known to be Mathis Gothart, called Nithart or Neithardt, the misnomer persists. Only about thirteen of his paintings have survived to the present day. The Isenheim altarpiece is his greatest work. He also, it is believed, painted the outer wings of a Dürer altarpiece at Frankfurt, which celebrates Mary's ascension, which was destroyed by fire.

Another contemporary of both Grünewald and Dürer, Hans Holbein the Younger, an ambitious painter who illustrated Martin Luther's translation of the Bible, who created a series of woodcuts called *The Dance of Death*, who, through Erasmus's recommendation to Saint Thomas More, came to paint many portraits of Henry VIII and his court, who supposedly used Grünewald's face for a crowned female saint, also painted an early optical illusion in *The Ambassadors*. In it we see two well-dressed men (one a noble, one a priest) standing before a table filled with musical and scientific instruments. Between the two men, hovering above the ground, is a strange amorphous shape. Only when one views the painting askance does the shape become clear: it is a skull. The painting predates the Dutch *vanitas* style by a century, yet seems clearly to be a *memento mori*, unless, as some have suggested, the skull is only a pun on the painter's name, which means "hollow bone."

ERIN'S PRAYERS

My friend Erin, when she was young, would kneel beside her bed each night to say her prayers. Unwilling to admit the possibility of dying before she awoke, she left her prayers unfinished, certain that God would see her through at least to her *amen*. I like the idea of sleep, dreams, tanglings in sheets and tossings and turnings, as prayer, caught up by the parenthesis of "Dear Heavenly Father," suspended, waiting for "Amen." I like the idea of story as saving grace, that Erin instinctively, intuitively discovered the scheme of Scheherazade, to leave off the ending to live another day.

To think that this entanglement of trivialities has lain dormant in my brain for years, gathering dust before it could gather strength, material, associations. Which is to say that as I sat half-listening to Brenda Miller read at the University of Utah, I was startled awake at the phrase *memento mori*, left dangling, it seemed, unexplained, unattached, and I wrote it on the back of Vin's note, and the phrase began to stitch together from my roiling sea of unorganized memories and thoughts yet another castigation on the literary world, another essay.

> The advantage of meditating on life and death is being able to say anything at all about them.
>
> E. M. CIORAN *All Gall Is Divided*

The danger of writing an essay like this: there is nowhere to end.

WAYNE MARINO

Soon after the Brenda Miller reading, I knew that this essay would end the morning before I took the SAT, when I rode my bike to the corner of Clemens Terrace and Emerson Drive and met John Ryan, who told me that Wayne Marino had died a few hours ago a few yards away. This was the same corner where I had, years earlier, wiped out on my bike and broken my top-front-left tooth, or had scraped the skin off my knuckles so badly that I still have scars; I can no longer recall which of those injuries happened that day, nor can I contort my hands into a handlebar grip that would rasp the left-hand knuckle against the detritus, the right hand scraping just above the wrist, where the scar is now hidden by hair; this was the day I got my retainer, and I was riding fast around the curve, leaning into it, and I was down before I realized that the loose bits of sand and rocks settled in the eddy of the street had it in for me.

I didn't much like Wayne Marino, though I barely knew him. It was more his crowd that I knew — Billy and Brian Basque and Brian Vogt, who lived down the street; Joey Marcantonio and his fat brother, Skinny Vinnie — brash and impetuous, peeling out on the street in their gray and brown primer-painted Camaros, smoking pot in the woods, punching me in the arm (this was Joey) when I wouldn't give up my seat next to John Ryan on the school bus. Wayne was like that: a showboat on the football field, an arrogant, swaggering maroon-and-white letter-jacket blur in the hallways at school, "waiting for the world's applause." So I shouldn't have cared much that he killed himself, crashed his black Mustang into the guardrail on Eden Lane, which was famous for its narrow, wrongly banked curves. But I cared, or I sensed that the news would haunt me beyond that afternoon as I took the SAT. It wasn't the #36 patch we wore on our football jerseys later that fall; it wasn't the black spray paint all over town — *Feel no pain, Wayne!*; it wasn't the girls with tears in their eyes. But perhaps it was death in my own backyard, in a place I knew, to a person barely older than I was. My grandparents had all died before I was born or when I was young, and though their deaths meant missing them, weeping in my mother's arms in the car on the way to the funeral, they never meant *it can happen to me*; I was too young to consider the existential repercussions of death or my connection to it. And no matter how I disliked Wayne, I never made the leap to *he deserved it*, even if he was drunk, even if he did drive fast, even if he thought he was immortal. I did, too — think I was immortal. I still am.

Bobby Russell, said John, had found him, awakened by the screech and crash just through his backyard. What is important to tell you about Bobby Russell? a) that he was nicknamed Cry Bobby; b) that he also listened to Rush, sometimes my cassettes of their early albums, which he didn't have; c) that one summer day he, John Ryan, and I were nailing together a tree fort deep in the woods, and Bobby fell, flew past me and John below, and landed with a thud flat on his back on a pile of scrap lumber — he gasped like a fish out of water, trying to catch his breath, and when John and I got down to him, we were astonished that he had managed to avoid the mutiny of nails jutting every which way and everywhere except where Bobby had fallen; d) that we never finished the fort, and its tree survived "progress" though most of its neighbors didn't: you can find it at the edge of the Eden Lane condominiums that sprawl where our woods used to be; the rungs we hammered into its trunk are slowly rotting away but still largely intact; e) that he lived at 13 Llewellyn Court and I lived at 13 Clemens Terrace, which meant that every now and then our parents would get each other's mail. By the time of the accident, I didn't see very much of Bobby, but I jumped inside his head for a moment to imagine finding the accordioned car, being unable to recognize the unmade driver, running back to call the police, trembling.

There were theories and rumors, of which I heard nothing until yesterday, when my best friend, Vin, and I watched a volleyball game at Brigham Young University, where I now work, and he explained that some people said that Wayne had had a spiritual crisis the weekend before he died while attending a local Catholic youth retreat called Antioch at Notre Dame Parish, across town. He didn't seem the type, I said. Yet there were rumors that upon his return from Antioch, he threw away his entire heavy metal collection, and that he may have crashed on purpose, committed suicide. I had heard none of this in high school. I hadn't even noticed inconsolable, withdrawn Deanna Belusko, the postmaster's daughter, who was just then beginning to date Wayne, who was to take her to the junior prom the following weekend, on what would be my seventeenth birthday. That evening when I turned seventeen I took Paige Chen, one of the long-ago mentioned pedants, to my junior prom. That afternoon after Wayne Marino died I took the SAT. Armed with my arsenal of Rush words, I got a 720 on the verbal section. This was important to me then.

An essay is an elaborated thing, composed over months, sometimes forgotten, set aside, returned to and revised. But who hath ears to hear, let him hear: that I am writing this essay exactly seventeen years later, to the day, having survived twice as long as I had then, been whirled through a universe of time and ideas so immeasurably fleet that it may be contained entirely within my memory and repassed, perhaps, in a moment, a sudden flash (and yet it is lived, and recounted, enumerated one story at a time). That now, as then, it is barely a day past the Patrickmas, which is the date I was to be born, according to the doctors, and which commemorates the death of my patron saint, for whom I am named, as is my father and his father before him and also many of our forebears, including him who left Ireland during the Great Hunger. That the calendar for March 2005, as I write, aligns exactly, day for date, with that of March 1988, half my life ago. That through some awkward, untoward coincidence, some fold in the expanding universe (and the navy's commitment to regularly relocate their personnel), I am once again with my boyhood best friend, whom I haven't seen in years; that our wives and our children are safe at my home, and for a moment I cannot remember myself then, seventeen years ago, and Vin, sitting beside me, is his spirit, never an eight-year-old boy in my class at Our Lady of Mercy, never a gangly teenage cross-country runner alongside John Ryan and John Anderson, never the young man dreaming of space who let me fend for myself at Notre Dame while he trained for the navy at Villanova; we are become our essences, detached from time and context, free from corruption and decay. And that on the anniversary of his death, Wayne Marino is remembered not only by his family, attending to the busy weekend crowd at their Birchwood Manor, preparing the horses, pausing, with a sharp turn, a look to the sky, his mother crossing herself, kissing the silver crucifix hanging about her neck, between the breasts that knew his suck (*My Lord and my God*, she begins . . .

Garlic

For twenty years, since the man he shared a fruit stand with stiffed him, my father-in-law has worked as a simple middle-man carting vegetables, mainly garlic, from Montevideo's giant central market to faraway cities and forgotten towns. He likes the easy pace of it, the chats with old friends at the market stalls, the quiet, jostling hours on the bus, the quick conversations with the terminal staff who watch his extra bags as he carries one slung over his shoulder to front-yard kiosks and corner bars, to steady customers who smile when they see him and offer him drinks and pay him when they can. He likes the card games and drinks at late hours in bars with fleeting friends his age and temperament who remember fatter times, and greener.

We left in the early morning, dressed in flannel and jeans, walked to the bus stop near his apartment: concrete slabs in patchy grass and rusting metal tubes holding up a corrugated fiberglass roof. Light from the street lamps overpowered the stars, or the clouds did, and crickets sang, or frogs, and a cat crossed our path and turned, paused, looked back menacingly, then continued on to the overflowing trash bins where it foraged for food, or slept. We waited in silence and yawns as other weary travelers arrived dressed in ties and slacks and dresses, yawning and silent and drab in the feeble light blocking stars and casting the world in dreary gray, and languor.

We hardly spoke, but I observed him, white with years and worn and wizened, his skin leather, his hands strong and curled from years of hauling his fifty-pound bags of garlic — I, unaccustomed and soft with tender hands and worsening eyesight from reading books and people.

The plot today is we are going to Mercado Modelo, Montevideo's central fruit and vegetable market, where he will buy garlic to sell and I will observe and accompany and sit lethargically on boxes of apples eating dried sausage on crackers and fry bread as the sun slashes through the spaces between easterly buildings.

He is, like so many other Uruguayan men, dressed in a plaid shirt and faded pants and comfortable *alpargatas*, canvas shoes with coiled-rope soles, with a white moustache and missing teeth. He is five-foot-eight but hunches over, he is overweight, he walks slowly and deliberately, sings ever so slightly when he talks, calls me *"mi hijo,"* my son, and watches the world with piercing steel-blue eyes.

On the bus, the people scattered to empty benches to sit alone, but my father-in-law and I sat with each other, his shoulder jabbing my biceps, in silence. After a short ride, we arrived at the Market, in the warehouse district in the middle of the city, north of the tall buildings, along Avenida José Batlle y Ordoñez, named after Uruguay's great social reformer president, who served twice in office from 1906 to 1910 and from 1916 to 1920. But the street name is ceremonial, perfunctory, and everyone calls the avenue by its old name, Propios, which means "ours" or "those who belong," because it once divided Us from Them. The Market is on the Ajenos side.

I was struck immediately by the immensity of the conglomeration of merchants, the hustle of runners with hand trucks dashing through amœbic crowds, the sweet and pungent smells of fruits in all stages of ripeness and decay, stacked neatly in piles and boxes or trampled underfoot. I saw colors and blurs of movement in the darkness turned back by vapor lights strung high from vaulted ceilings. I heard echoes of a more glorious past

grown too big and past its limits in the stalls and stands sprawled outside the original fading central building into smaller buildings and spilled over into alleyways and walkways, among the trucks and tarps and stacks and stacks of crates and boxes, everywhere.

I thought of the impossible complexity of interrelations. I grew up near New York City, forty-five minutes west in suburban New Jersey. Life was simplified and compartmentalized for me and — for the trees or for the regimen, I cannot tell — I never had to see far beyond my neighborhood or my schoolwork, and because I was good at school, I never worried. Life was a series of assignments and tests and time to play with friends, and home was stable and never wanting. I excelled in math and science, and our high school science experiments were contained, assumed a closed system, and we spoke lightly of the unreality of a closed system, or of the problem of working within a system to test that system, as scientists must inescapably do, but it was theory, and reality was neat and ordered and I believed I could wrap my mind around it.

But New York, it seemed to me little by little and increasingly as I grew older and visited more frequently and paid more attention to the local news on television, was chaos with a veneer of order. It was a sphere atop a cone, waiting for the slightest provocation to send it careening down to destruction. Simple things — the garbage collection for so many people and businesses, the sanitation, the subway system maintenance — were incredibly complex, things I could never fit inside my brain. I considered the weight of buildings and people supported by the island, perforated like Swiss cheese by subway and sewer tunnels. I thought of the apartment buildings just inside Manhattan on the Upper West Side, where the George Washington Bridge empties out and which Interstate 95 dives underneath in a series of short tunnels on its way to the Bronx. Do the people above — watching television, doing homework — know that their building rests only on columns of concrete and rebar? The engineers have it all figured out, I realize, and the buildings remain standing, but my amazement at that fact always gets the better of me, and something like an irrational fear grips me as I drive underneath them.

A List, in Spanish, of the Various Fruits and Vegetables Available at Different Times of the Year at Mercado Modelo, as Given Me by My Father-in-Law Some Months after Our Visit to the Market:

> papa, boñato, zapallo, calabaza, zapallito, berenjena
> blanca y negra, cebolla blanca, morrón rojo y amarillo, [My
> computer automatically changes morrón to moron and
> capitalizes Amarillo. That we allow our programmers to
> insert such annoying functions in our software I take
> as a sign of increasing dependence on machines and
> willingness to surrender decisions and avoid thinking
> or knowing useful conventions.] remolacha, zanahoria,
> espinaca, acelga, escarola, lechuga verde crespa, lechuga
> manteca, lechuga morada, lechuga morada crespa, brocoli,

coliflor, radicha, zalsifi, nabo, nabiza, puerro, apio, repollo
blanco, repollo morado, repollo crespo, cebollín, albahaca,
perejil, hongos, espárragos, eudibias, brotes de soja, brotes
de alfalfa, choclo, repollitos de bruselas, ajos, pepinos,
tomates, arvejas, habas, porotos manteca frescos, chauchas,
chaucha alubia, cebolla colorada, sandía, melón, kiwi,
naranjas, tanjarines, bergamotas, pomelo rosado, pomelo
amarillo, bananas, frutillas, uva blanca, uva moscatel
rosada, uva chinche, higos, manzana delicia, manzana grani
smith, manzana redelicia, kinotos, peras, duraznos rey del
monte, duraznos pelón, damascos, durazno blanco, ciruela
betellita, ciruela morada, ciruela blanca, gemidas, cerezas,
frambuesas, ananá [not the typical Spanish word for
pineapple, but the one Uruguayans use and share with
German and Russian and Latvian and, I suspect, many
other languages].

My father once told me about Robert Shields, a retired minister
who tried to keep a journal of everything he did. At the time,
it seemed to me a colossal waste of time, but I didn't ponder
the impossibility of it all until later. I imagine that he hadn't
read Jorge Luis Borges's "The Library of Babel," or maybe he
had and hadn't felt the despair and futility of the idea of com
pleteness or total self-reflexivity, metaliterature, writing about
writing about writing trapped forever unable to write more
than "I am writing, still writing, writing, writing still" never
doing except writing caught in an infinite loop like Aureliano
Babilonia at the end of *One Hundred Years of Solitude* reading
the moment he is living unable to escape the broken record
looping and looping while his town is obliterated and he goes
on reading, only reading.

The personal essay mimics the activity of a mind at work. It
reflects discovery through writing. Its author better not begin

with a conclusion or epiphany already in hand. And yet, of course an essay is artifice, somewhat inspired by the muse and somewhat formed by conscious decision and revision and pruning to finally appear fresh and reflexive of a mind at work. Yet, this seems to me also an impossibility. One must restrain oneself, heed the lesson of Apollo's son Phaethon: rein the horses one can, avoid the horses one can't.

An essay is performative if its medium — words, sentences, tone, diction, format, style — reflects its subject. Yet: an essay that ends up being *about* chaos or entropy?

I wonder if he gets bored, walking alone so much of the time with his bags of garlic. I wonder what he thinks about, or does he think very little? is he simply content to be? When I walk, I walk to reach my destination. I am ashamed of my walks, purposeful beasts, in light of Thoreau and Hazlitt and now Sebald and so many other great walkers whose time was consecrated to the what-have-you, the come-what-may of a walk. I have bought into the hustle and bustle of everyday life in America, getting and getting to, arriving. Neil Peart writes, echoing the spirit of so many who came before, "The point of the journey is not to arrive." And yet for me, it is. And I am ashamed of that.

Still, my father-in-law *does* walk to get to destinations. He arrives at bars and grocery stores and restaurants and kiosks to sell garlic. Yet, I see him not as an acquisitive product-oriented destination seeker like me. He is somehow above that, halfway translated to a calm oneness with the world around him. I say this because he never complains, because he moves about quietly and sometimes stares fixedly at nothing, as if lost in thought or at peace. But I also remember men who worked their whole adult lives in a tire factory that I withstood only one summer. They, too, seemed to have that resigned look in their eyes, and I imagined it was their escape from the atrophy of routine, from the heat of the tire ovens and the black dust of the air. My difficulty was my resistance: I couldn't not think and be miserable longing for variety and excitement and, I would have said, it was mind-numbing, and so perhaps their minds had been numbed, and the younger men spoke incessantly of the weekend and the lottery and of everything that was not work and would make work no longer necessary.

I have no proof that my father-in-law, whose walks are also determined by the market and his small part in it as distributor of garlic to small markets and restaurants in faraway towns, walks any differently than I do. I have no proof that he is anything like the ideal I paint of him with his peace and oneness with the landscape of the country he's lived in for almost seventy years.

He tells his past very infrequently, but when he tells, he explains that he was raised in the farmland north of the capital by humble parents whose struggle to live meant that children were expected to help with chores and planting and harvest. Early on, he was an exceptional student, his children tell me. In the sixth grade, his teacher gave him a dictionary, which she signed, "To Uber, Best of luck in your future studies. You will do well." But his father needed him at home and he never went back to school. When I ask him about it, his voice seems a lament, but his words remain stoic with the inevitable fact of life in the 1940s in Uruguay where land reforms and social programs were enough to make people like his parents content to be working their own farm and in control of their own progress and prosperity.

Almost simultaneously, as I write, there appear in my mind two phrases, one from Lu Hsun and one from John Lennon. Respectively: "This, too, is life," and "Life is what happens to you while you're busy making other plans."

Fig. 10.

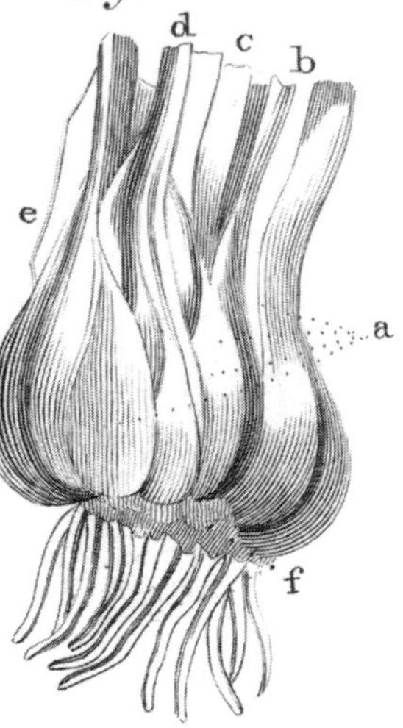

Garlic, historians believe, was originally native to mountainous eastern Asia, and was traded widely so that the earliest farmers, in Mesopotamia, cultivated it ten thousand years ago. The Greek historian Herodotus wrote of a memorial plaque dating from about 2500 BC on the Great Pyramid of Cheops at Giza that mentioned the cost of the radishes, onions, and garlic used to feed workers. When Tutankhamen's tomb was opened in 1922, archeologists found among the artifacts therein six dried cloves of garlic. In about 1500 BC the Children of Israel, recently escaped from slavery in Egypt, remembered wistfully the fish, cucumbers, melons, leeks, onions, and garlic they used to eat. It has long been a staple, if a disparaged one, because of its breath-fouling effects.

All garlic is of one species, *allium sativar*, though bulbs do differ widely from one another in size, shape, texture, and other ways. Variations are called cultivars. In this way, it occurs to me, garlic is like people. Its Latin name, which has filtered into its common name in French, Italian, and Spanish, may derive from a Celtic term for "burning," and it shares a genus with onions, chives, shallots, and leeks. This last contributed to garlic's English name, along with the Anglo-Saxon word *gar*, which is a lance or spear: gar-leek, because of its spear-shaped stalk, reminiscent of a leek's.

Garlic has also been called, derogatorily, "poor man's treacle" or "churl's treacle," *treacle* being an antidote or cure-all, and *churl* being that ill-bred lowest class of freeman who has, it seems, the last laugh. While aristocracy from Persia to Spain despised the herb and forbad their courtiers to partake of it, recent research confirms some of what ancient Egyptian,

Chinese, Indian, and Mediterranean "common" peoples have long believed about garlic's curative properties. Garlic can lower cholesterol and decrease a person's risk of getting certain cancers. Louis Pasteur, in 1858, discovered its antibacterial properties, and its diluted juices were used as an antiseptic during World War I.

> Garlic then have power to save from death
> Bear with it though it makes unsavoury breath.
>
> <div align="right">JOHN HARRINGTON <i>The Englishman's Doctor</i></div>

We are slow and methodical in our research nowadays, taking great pains to reduce or eliminate outside uncontrolled influences on our subjects, so it may take us a while to confirm or refute the ancients' claims that garlic also stimulates the heart, fights rheumatism, and cures headaches, dog bites, earaches, intestinal worms, and throat tumors.

Every three months or so, my father-in-law brings home a fresh braid of large garlic bulbs tied with a red ribbon. He hangs it on a nail just outside the kitchen doorway for good luck, savory food, and health.

Once, as we rode standing in the back of a rusted pickup along a long dirt road north of Montevideo, my father-in-law spoke about his family, his wife's unpredictable temper, his son Fernando's bureaucratic tangles caught between the bike factory that had laid him off temporarily and the government that refused to pay him temporary unemployment benefits. He spoke about his happiness for Karina, my wife, though she lived far away and they saw each other only rarely. He spoke with pride about his daughter Graciela, who had recently graduated from the university and would be an elementary school teacher, though she had forgotten her ID on the day of the incoming teacher examination, had been unable to take it, and was thus relegated to substitute work for a year because all teachers are processed through the state system, not hired through interviews and common accord.

And then — how did we get here? — an allusion to his oldest son, Bernardo, called Lalo, his firstborn. He had played soccer in the minor leagues, and as a young man had stood his father down those nights when he came home broke, drunk, belligerent; he had gone into the military for the sake of a steady paycheck and for the sake of his mother, who worked a factory job to keep the family afloat while her husband pissed away his own earnings in the cantinas of the Interior; he had excelled in marksmanship and horsemanship, earning an instructor's job at the training center in Colonia along with a blue-blood golden-boy sonofatorturer who was always a second behind, always a bit off the mark, except for the evening he shot and killed Lalo with one bullet, claiming it was a gun-cleaning accident and getting off, despite witnesses who heard him shouting, threatening. Now Lalo's military pension, ascended to that of a lieutenant's and awarded posthumously to his mother, keeps the family comfortable enough in these days of hardships and factory closings and my father-in-law returning home having sold only half his stock.

He says, "I've been through a lot. You know."

I do. The pause sits heavily, holding to the truck as it thrums, the whipping wind too feeble to lift it and carry it away.

The impossible complexity of interrelations, commerces, supplies and demands and imports and exports, middlemen and middlemen and an accessible price when the fruit is spit out the other end before I buy it, before I bite it. And only one thread, garlic, almost impossible to follow from a poor farmer in China during Uruguay's off-season when garlic must be imported, to an assembly line of women braiding bulbs together by their long spear leaves, to a man stacking strands between sheets of purple paper in cardboard boxes with *garlic* written in seven languages, to a boat across the ocean to a port in Montevideo to awaiting trucks to be stacked and delivered across town in the early morning hours to a stall in the Market, bustling below the grayness of the night amidst the clanking of carts and crunching of boxes and the colors, laid on slats of wood in one of the rows and rows of labyrinthine paths, awaiting my father-in-law or somebody like him, to be carried in fifty-pound bags in the underside of a bus from Montevideo to Rocha then distributed a few strands at a time to front-yard kiosks and corner bars to be sold to the customers to be used in the sauce for the pasta, for sustenance, good health and good luck, at tonight's dinner.

Ego Vici Mundum

One evening in my hotel room in Buenos Aires (I was there for a weeklong conference; I was living in Montevideo, Uruguay, at the time), my left-top-front tooth broke (dentists avoid the directional adjectives, calling the tooth "number 9"; seek ye resonances in the *White Album*). Really it was a piece of filling that broke away, returning me to the day, almost two decades before, when I was playing "spud" with the other kids in my neighborhood, running full speed down the street in front of my house, when a kid shouted "Spud!" Frank Lepore stopped suddenly in front of me, I tripped, and I fell face first to the asphalt, eating the street. Mothers a block away heard my howl.

The tooth-colored filling I got the next day lasted nineteen years, until I was a graduate student at Ohio University. The one I got to replace it (paying for it myself; I had no dental insurance) lasted only one year. Now, alone in South America, still without insurance, I would have to replace it again. I had no recourse at the Ohio dentist whose shoddy work had failed me so quickly. Worried about the prospect of a visit to an unknown dentist in Uruguay, I was returned to a series of days almost a decade earlier when, as a Mormon missionary in Montevideo, I went to a Mormon dentist who would fill a cavity for free. His name was Adolfo Pérez; he was blond with blue eyes; he lived and worked very near the "Jewish Neighborhood," near where Arenal Grande becomes Justicia. I thought: Those drill bits look too big. I thought, too: Strange that *Adolfo* (meaning "noble wolf") is not taboo here in Uruguay. I think, now: And yet, why need it be? Saint Adolf of Osnabrück, a thirteenth-century German bishop, dedicated his life to serving the poor. Saint Adolphus Ludigo-Mkasa was put to death by the king of Uganda in 1885 simply for being a Christian. Saint Adolphus of Seville was also martyred, with his brother, in 850, by a local Muslim ruler. Adolphus Busch, a nineteenth-century German immigrant to the United States, was the first brewer to pasteurize his beer. Adolph Coors, another beer magnate, kept his business alive through Prohibition by producing malted milk and ceramics. All of these had the name before Hitler.

But after Hitler? After the Shoah, millions and millions of people herded and gassed, Nazis hell-bent on Adolf Eichmann's "final solution," children across Europe sent to their deaths by bureaucrats seeking to save their own skins? (Execrable Eichmann, I remember, expatriated to Buenos Aires to farm rabbits, among other things, before he was exposed, extradited, executed.) I had never met an Adolf of any kind before that dentist. Internet name trackers (for the United States) confirm a sharp drop-off in the name's popularity, from 158th in the 1890s to a virtual nonentity in the 1940s. (In fairness, the Spanish Adolfo has appeared in the top 600 recently.) Then I thought: Latin Americans still call their children Jesus, too. So maybe this is a healthy recognition that a name has many bearers; perhaps it is a refusal to allow one man to monopolize a good word.

Those early fall days in Buenos Aires, as I rode buses around town with my smile in my pocket, hiding my chipped tooth, I noticed blue-and-white bills posted everywhere for presidential candidate Adolfo Rodriquez Saá and his running mate Melchor Posse, and my mind turned to the three priests from the East, bearing their gifts across the desert, following that star to one of the world's many Jesuses. I thought I had remembered T. S. Eliot's "The Journey of the Magi," and would have written now of his conversion, quoted a few lines that resonate with my time in Buenos Aires, to connect the Epiphany to the epiphany I am aiming for in this essay, such as "the cities hostile and the towns unfriendly / And the villages dirty" or

> We returned to our places, . . .
> But no longer at ease

but I was wrong. Nowhere in his poem does Eliot mention Melchior (nor Gaspar nor Balthasar), names handed us by tradition at least as old as the seventh century. Perhaps I remembered, instead, Carman Bliss's "The Sending of the Magi," with its

> Melchior, the seer
> Who read the starry plan;

I don't know. From somewhere now lost to me I received the connection between *Melchor* (meaning "king city") and the three kings, who came from afar to honor the king of kings, who went home another way, so as not to betray the child to Herod, who would have taken and killed him.

Every Thursday afternoon between three-thirty and four, the grandmothers of the disappeared (they were mothers of the disappeared, too, once, but they have given up that hope) march in circles around the Plaza de Mayo, front of the Catedral Metropolitana, front of the Casa Rosada, seat of government, from whose balconies Evita rallied the *descamisados,*

the shirtless, before her death at age thirty-three. The women shuffle in their white shawls, in silent protest to the government that knows, to leaders and dealers left over from nearly a decade of "dirty war": military rule, midnight raids, tortures and assassinations, and the trade in infants across the borders with Uruguay and Chile.

Among so many who lost children and grandchildren: Juan Gelman, the poet, who was not home when they came for him, whose son and daughter-in-law were taken; Juan Gelman, whose son ended up in a barrel in the river Luján, a bullet in the back of the head; Juan Gelman, whose pregnant *nuera*— (see how the word in Spanish avoids the coldness of English legalspeak? see how the word suggests two: *no era*, "she wasn't," "she no longer existed"?)—was taken to the Hospital Militar in Montevideo, where she gave birth, then was killed. This much we now know. The child was given to a policeman whose wife was barren. This story again and again: pregnant women taken, raped, tortured, executed, their babies kidnapped. This story from Argentina. This story from Uruguay. This story from Chile. Military men who went on Sundays to church, on Mondays to the machine, to beat and prod and submerge and shock and threaten. Juan Gelman, the poet, self-exiled to Mexico, in an open letter to his grandchild, published in 1995:

> On the one hand I have always found repugnant the idea of your calling "Daddy" some military or police gangster who stole you, or some friend of those who assassinated your father. On the other hand I have always wished that in whatever home you may have grown up you were well brought up and educated and loved a lot. Still, I have always thought there must be some hole, or failure in the love shown you . . . because they would have to have some awareness of your story and how they were involved in falsifying it. I suppose that you have been lied to a lot. Then, too, I have wondered all these years what I would do if you were found—whether to drag you out of the home you knew; whether to speak with your adoptive parents and establish visiting rights, always on the basis of your knowing who you were and where you came from. The dilemma came up and circled around time and time again, whenever the possibility arose that the Grandmothers of the Plaza de Mayo had found you.

(The Grandmothers, whose work other days of the week is re-membering, re-constituting families, who dedicate their time to pestering government officials, pressuring the press, searching in archives and unmarked graves, did find Macarena, as they had found over seventy children before her, and Gelman was returned to his granddaughter in March 2000. She was twenty-three years old, living in Montevideo. Her mother's remains have not yet been found.)

It was during this time of continental conflict, fallen democracies, fierce disappearances, that Adolfo Pérez Esquivel organized Servicio Paz y Justicia in Buenos Aires (and then elsewhere in Latin America), prevailed on the United Nations to establish a Human Rights Commission, was imprisoned without cause, then released under a sort of insile, under restrictions and obligatory visits to the police. He kept at it, reclaiming and rebuking his government, organizing people. In 1980, in his speech to the Nobel committee that had awarded him its Peace Prize, he said:

> I speak of my own Argentina where situations have led to systems of injustice that . . . have resulted in the murdered, the injured, the disappeared, the tortured, imprisoned, and exiled.
>
> This situation, anguished and unjust, is . . . felt with sorrow by the families of the disappeared, and especially the mothers, like the mothers of the Plaza de Mayo whose valorous and international action for peace is a patient witness bearing the sorrow of uncertainty about the fate of their children.

The grandmothers were not walking this day, a Monday in early April, feast day of Saint Epiphanius, as my own country continued its invasion of Iraq, and Adolfo Pérez Esquivel sent impassioned letters to George W. Bush, accusing: "You have neither capacity nor courage to open your mind and your spirit to compassion"; and comparing: "You say you pray to God and you believe you are predestined for humanity. Hitler had the same thoughts when he unleashed his madness." As I walked about the Plaza de Mayo, I kept my eyes fixed, sidestepped the dirty women languishing under the columns in front of the cathedral doors, turned briskly to loose my garment from the grip of one who said, "Please, anything you have, God bless

you," eluded another who moved into my path. I half-saw signs
scrawled with statistics and sad stories. My downcast eyes
scanned the frayed flannel edges of blankets, then returned
to tracing the grout between the stones.

I entered the cathedral to escape the rabble. In my head
swirled the story of this silver land on its silver river: this unbelievable, this brutal, methodical, mechanical, cold, unfeeling,
this rage for order, this Process of National Reorganization, this
maniacal torture of misidentity: children kidnapped, scattered,
unknowing. It was a story I barely knew, knew only in broken
ideas and images, my own imagination's impositions on a history that had been hidden from me, ignored, nevertalkedof. I
wondered if their very DNA might carry within it some inkling
of who they were, if they might have tendencies to seek justice
for the downtrodden, as their parents had done. I hoped for
heated arguments between them and their "parents" whose ide-
ologies must have been at polar odds with their parents. Inside
the cathedral it was almost silent. I saw the ornate arches, the
wrought-iron railings, the velvet chairs, the silver-plated altar,

the faded frescoes, the gilded window work, the guarded tomb of José San Martin, liberator of Argentina, Chile, and Peru, born in rural Yapeyú, Argentina, of stately parents, educated in Europe, returned to set his people free. In a moment of calm, I cast my eyes upward forty meters to the cupola. There engraved, in Roman characters, I read the title of this essay: EGO VICI MUNDUM. It was all I could see within the rim.

Even before I could puzzle out its meaning, translate those words (think Freud, Caesar, French newspaper), I understood what it meant, and not only what it meant but where it came from, who had said it, about what, and why. Jerome's Vulgate translation of John 16:33 reads, more completely: *In mundo pressuram habebitis: sed confidite, ego vici mundum,* which is to say, "In the world ye shall have tribulation; but be of good cheer. I have overcome the world."

This was not the solution, a revelation for the revolution; this was not justice delayed and eternal rewards; it was no opiate. It was, perhaps, some sudden pull behind the heart, some opening to compassion, some inscrutable calm regardless, despite it all.

I left then. Buoyed in spirit, or introspective in mind, I walked out the cathedral doors, past the fliers in the foyers, beside the benedicted mendicants, among the twelve Corinthian columns that grow from south to north as the earth drops away to the river-sea, close to the crest calling out SALVUM FAC POPULUM TUUM, into the good airs. I did not notice then the relief watching over me in the pediment above, but I have learned it since:

In that gable gaze sheep and cattle, calm camels in the corners above the cornices, upon a reunion scene: ten repentant brothers and the brother they had disappeared, who was lost then found, dead then alive, sold by his siblings to Egypt to

be a slave, turned their savior in time of famine. There is Jacob
returned to his son Joseph: Israel's son is revealed, the ten are
relieved, Benjamin released. In this everlasting embrace the
father and the son keep watch over the plaza: the speeches
and protests, marchers and merchants, the weekly silent pro-
cession of old women in kerchiefs keeping vigil, searching,
remembering.

Gravity and Distance

I believe that it's best to be straightforward about things. The metaphor I am invoking with this essay's title is borrowed from a song by Rush:

> Gravity and distance change the passage of light
> Gravity and distance change the color of right.
>
> NEIL PEART "The Color of Right"

The lyrics that surround it seem to cast these lines in the sense of "don't be self-righteous," but, of course, the metaphor also plays on the double sense of gravity and distance, physical vs. metaphysical. I take the quotation as another way of saying there is a great difference between theory and practice. When things are serious, when we see them up close, they look different.

We start with Montaigne, 1533–92, father of the essay form, collector of thoughts in commonplace books, quotes from the sages, marginalia expanded to his grandiose discussion of himself, coiner of the term, in French, *essais*, meaning "attempts" or "trials," widely read for his honesty, his wit, his invitation to accompany him in thought as he ponders a variety of life questions.

His influence was felt widely in his day, even as it is now. Follow the line of influence to Pascal, 1623–62, mathematician, scientist, inventor of the first digital computing machine, found by his father deriving Euclid at age eleven, convert to Jansenism, apologist author of the never-completed fragmentary *Pensées*, a rational argument for the necessity of belief and the truth of Christ's message and salvation, written, apparently, in reaction to, against, with a copy of Montaigne's *Essais* in hand.

Skip a few centuries to Simone Weil, 1909–43, born in affluence in Paris, raised Jewish, critic of capitalism, teacher of the poor, mercenary in Spain's civil war, field hand and factory worker alongside those she struggled to support, near convert to Catholicism, social critic, saint of all outsiders, author of, among other things, *Gravity and Grace* and *Waiting for God*, written with Pascal in hand and in a similarly fragmented style.

Among countless others whose writings have been guided by these three I place myself, rather audaciously, 1971–, husband, father, bachelor of physics, doctor of English, inventor of nothing substantial, collector of scattered thoughts, lover of metaphor, not French, convert to Mormonism, writing with Montaigne, Pascal, and Weil in hand, scattered on the desk, on the floor, on the bed behind me.

Sixteen-thirties, Pisa, Italy: (according to legend) Galileo drops various objects from the Leaning Tower and observes that they land at approximately the same time.

The acceleration of gravity, g, equals nine point eight meters per second squared; thirty-two feet per second per second.

Sixteen eighty-seven, *Mathematical Principles of Natural Philosophy*, Sir Isaac Newton: "Every particle in the universe attracts every other particle with a force that is directly proportional to the product of their masses and inversely proportional to the square of the distance between them."

The universal gravitational constant, the number inside the proportional, G, equals six point six seven two times ten to the negative eleventh Newton (kilogram meter per second squared) meters squared per kilogram squared.

August 7, 1971, four and a half months after my birth, astronaut David Scott is on the moon; in the absence of air resistance he drops the proverbial falcon's feather and geologist's hammer, and they reach the moon's surface simultaneously.

Muttered under his breath after Galileo is forced to retract his Ptolemaic heliocentric views before an Inquisition tribunal:

E pur si muove.
(But it does move.)

This can't be the first conflict between faith and science, but it is early enough for me to choose it as epitomal. I see the conflict as born of egotism and corruption. *I enjoy my position of power; I claim that God has put me here; in order to stay where I am, I must keep the people down.* I have educated myself; I see that the world does not work the way you say it does, the way the scriptures say; I have no need of your religion, your stories, your oppressive God. *Deny what you know; bow down and worship; confirm what the scripture says.* But it does move.

With only minor variations, people respond to the news that I've left behind a bachelor's degree in physics to pursue a master's and a PhD in English in the same way: "That's a big switch." We're used to one or the other. Science or Art. Right or left brain.

The inevitable Q: "What made you decide to change from physics to English?"

Being a chemist in the world's eyes, and feeling . . .
a writer's blood in my veins.

PRIMO LEVI The Monkey's Wrench

It seems pretentious to claim "a writer's blood" in my own veins, but I think Levi's evocation fits. Unlike many people you read about, I never had an epiphany in my youth about my calling in life. The priests and nuns who taught me in grade school often mused about their callings — still, small voices that told them to dedicate their lives to the Lord, never get married, live in poverty. I grew up afraid. "What if God calls me to be a priest?" I wondered, knowing that you can't refuse God. Even before I liked girls I was repelled by the thought of lifelong celibacy.

Thankfully, God never did call me to be a priest, and instead I went through phases of interests that changed according to what was going on around me and what I was learning. When I started playing Little League I wanted to be a baseball player, never mind the fact that I never got a hit in a game. When my friends and I started listening to rock and roll, I bought a guitar and learned to play. I took part in all the activities my parents could handle, did well in my classes, in swimming, track and field, and football, and enjoyed learning. The most long-lived of my (serious) possible future vocations were archaeology, inspired by the dinosaur books my mother bought me and later by the Indiana Jones movies; architecture, because of my father's advice about combining my drawing ability with a realistic career and because of *The Fountainhead*; and physics, because of a wonderful high school teacher whose approach to science was experimental and mechanistic and the world made sense and it was good, and because of my own ego. My father had told me that physics was the most difficult major, and I wanted to prove that I could learn it.

I graduated from Notre Dame in 1993 with my BS in physics, somewhat soured on the idea of continuing on into the higher, weirder realms of science, and I soon left the country to serve a two-year mission for my new church. I had become a Mormon during my junior year, and the idea of spreading the news and serving others in a foreign country was appealing. I was sent to Uruguay, where I learned Spanish, met my wife, worked hard, sweated and froze, and did a lot of thinking.

It was during that time that I finally decided that I wouldn't continue in physics — shut out so many interests and activities for the sake of a paycheck. I *could* do it, sit around for hours crunching through problems and grasping at theories, but I didn't want to. I had gotten good grades in physics, I passed my tests, and my experiments gave close to their intended results. But I had already started realizing by the time I was a sophomore, and physics was beyond Newton's deterministic universe and onto things I could no longer see, that I was no longer so taken with science. I began then taking English classes and philosophy classes and theology classes; by my senior year I was taking painting and figure drawing and photography classes; I played more volleyball than anything else. Physics was too limiting, too theoretical, too exclusive. I wanted to think about other things, play the guitar, sing I wanted, like everyone does, to work at something variable and self-directed, something I loved doing; I wanted to earn enough to support a family, wake up excited to go to work, do something I'd do for free anyway, that sort of thing.

We search for other lives that parallel our own. It is comforting to know we are not alone. I like to see the similarities between my father and me. We have the same name (something like living with a nominal twin: mostly problematic but once or twice useful: frequent flier miles, roadside assistance). We have nearly the same voice (also problematic when callers ask for Pat). We are both tall and strong. We look alike, except for my father's moustache, glasses, and darker, grayer hair. We have the same difficulty with sticking to science and math at the expense of the humanities.

During his college years at Notre Dame, my father studied chemical engineering but also sang in the glee club and learned to play Beatles songs on guitar. Midway through his senior year, in the middle of a sort of existential dilemma, he decided to throw away the three and a half years he had already spent on engineering and change his major to music. Final exams for fall semester were after Christmas, but he didn't go back; he stayed working for an uncle pouring concrete basements in Milwaukee, then worked selling portable Whirlpool baths. Then his draft number came up and it was too late to get back into school to avoid the army. He spent the summer in basic training in Missouri, some days so hot the troops spent all day in an air conditioned movie theater, then moved on to New Jersey for electronics repair training, anything to postpone the trip to Vietnam. Saturdays he spent in New York at Cardinal Spellman's Servicemen's Club — no alcohol, just pool and ping-pong and local Catholic girls, among them my mother. After Vietnam, after his counterpart, the day-shift guy in the signal corps, got blown up by a grenade, after his mother fell terribly ill with cancer, after his reprimand on counts of subversion for publishing an antiwar newspaper on base in Chicago, after he and my mother were married, he returned to Notre Dame, talked his way out of his failing grades, retook some classes, and finished his degree in chemical engineering. A few years ago, he retired after thirty years with Exxon.

As the beneficiary of that self-sacrificial decision to stick with the sure thing, to become an engineer and find a job and work for thirty years with the same company to give his family a comfortable life, I respect his choice. And he still sings, but I can't help wondering what he might have done with music. At times I lament the choice he made, wonder if he felt he had to make it, if he compared his possibilities to those his salesman father had, if he felt his ability constituted a responsibility to society; I wonder if I, not yet born but in his near future, swayed his decision with the weight of my needs. When he was a young father he still played his guitar and taught me "Day Tripper," but now only my brothers and I ever pick it up to play.

His brother Jeff did choose music, and he plays guitar as well as anyone I've heard. Their mother died when Jeff was seventeen, their father was always on the road selling something, my father was married and living in New Jersey, their brother Tom was off at college then off on a mission for his new Mormon church, so Jeff and the youngest, Lynne, ended up fending for themselves. Jeff drinks, he sleeps in, gets fired, gets married, gets divorced, studies refrigeration and air conditioning, quits, thinks he's being followed, thinks he's the victim, thinks there's no way back, joins a band, misses a gig, doesn't pay his rent, moves to Reno, shacks up, dyes his hair blonde. He's gone for years, no phone, nobody has his address, then he calls "Hey I got a job driving trucks and I'm a couple miles away. Come pick me up?" or he calls for money, then he's gone again.

All the natural movements of the soul are controlled by laws analogous to those of physical gravity.

SIMONE WEIL *Gravity and Grace*

Other useful metaphors from the realm of science and mathematics:

$$\Delta x \Delta p \geq \hbar$$

It is fundamentally impossible to make simultaneous measurements of a particle's position and velocity with infinite accuracy: "Since the measuring device has been constructed by the observer . . . we have to remember that what we observe is not nature in itself but nature exposed to our method of questioning." Werner Heisenberg, 1927, much for science, more for metaphor and a postmodern mindset of doubt.

$$f(x) = x^2 - \mu$$

"Many important spatial patterns of Nature are either irregular or fragmented to such an extreme degree that classical geometry is hardly of any help in describing their form. . . . It is possible in many cases to remedy this absence of geometric representation by using a family of shapes I propose to call fractals." Benoit Mandelbrot, 1977, advanced geometry of infinite complexities: mountain ranges, holes in cheese, rivers and streams, veins in leaves, the circulatory system, immeasurable coastline, if you measure on the scale of a grain of sand.

$$F_n = F_{n-1} + F_{n-2}: 0, 1, 1, 2, 3, 5, 8, 13, 21, 34, \text{ ad infinitum}$$

"A certain man put a pair of rabbits in a place surrounded on all sides by a wall. How many pairs of rabbits can be produced from that pair in a year if it is supposed that every month each pair begets a new pair which from the second month on becomes productive?" Leonardo de Pisa/filius Bonacci/Fibonacci, 1202, contemporary of Francis of Assisi, brought base-ten Arabic number system to Europe; the Fibonacci set of numbers accurately describes the number of sections in spiral shells, the number of kernels on a corncob, the number of peas in a pod, the number of leaves in a cluster on a branch, and various other patterns found in nature.

$$\frac{\partial^2 \Psi}{\partial x^2} = -\frac{2m}{\hbar^2}(E-U)\Psi$$

$$E = mc^2$$

Einstein said, "I, at any rate, am convinced that [God] does not throw dice," and yet quantum theory and relativity remain in force as mutually exclusive, mutually beneficial and provable principles. In the search for a grand unified theory of physics, these two are insurmountable obstacles. If Einstein is right, completely right, then Schrödinger is wrong, and vice versa. Though most people would be hard-pressed to explain exactly how, Einstein's theory manifest its power to the world in Hiroshima. Schrödinger and Dirac's work has made its mark more subtly. After all, where Einstein is known the world over for his contributions to physics, Schrödinger is best known for his possibly dead cat.

From a letter from a friend alerting me to another friend's deteriorating health and hospitalization: "*Es bastante grave.*" Spanish. *Es* means "is"; in Spanish, which often casually omits sentence subjects because of separate distinguishable verb conjugations, *es* can mean "it is"; *it*, in the context of this letter, means "the situation" or "the illness." *Bastante* means "enough" or "sufficient"; used as a modifier it may also mean "very"; I know of no English cognate. *Grave* means "grave."

Grave is an overlap. Gravity, the force of attraction, the force holding us to earth's surface, cause of the apple falling. Gravity, the seriousness of the situation, the bleak outlook, the lack of hope. Grave, the adjective form of hopelessness, danger, heaviness. Grave, the end, a hole in the ground, one with the earth, pulling the others.

gravamen (grievance), grave[1] (place of burial), grave[2] (serious, weighty), grave[3] (carve, engrave), grave[4] (remove barnacles and coat with pitch), grave[5] (slowly, solemnly), graveclothes (shroud), gravedigger (digger of graves), gravel (rock fragments), gravelblind (purblind), graven image (idol), graver (stone carver), grave robber (tomb plunderer), gravestone (tombstone), graveyard (cemetery), graveyard shift (midnight to 8:00 a.m.), gravid (pregnant), gravimeter (instrument used to determine specific gravity), graving dock (dock where ships are cleaned), gravitate (sink, settle, approach), gravitation (attraction between masses), graviton (quantum of attraction), gravity[1] (attraction between masses), gravity[2] (seriousness, importance), gravure (intaglio printing), gravy (sauce for meats)

I loved Gonzalo, my gravely ill friend. I had seen him suffering with cancer, learning English and computers and cooking, singing along, teaching me lyrics in Spanish, me teaching him lyrics in English, riding around town on the yellow wheelchair motorcycle the Rotary Club gave him, unable to move his legs, steering his bicycle-riding brother into ditches, always smiling, the typical elegiac praise you come up with for people who've got it tough, I'm not doing him any favors making him into a cliché of the happy cripple, the inspiring example, but that is *my* weakness, not his. He was vibrant. We were the same age, Gonzalo and I; we liked the same music. Wednesdays we rode away from town to the beaches talking and laughing, Gonzalo confined to his chair.

Then I was far away in the United States and he in Uruguay, and my prayers went unanswered. I dashed off a letter, filled

it with memories and hope, struggled to inspire from a distance, never thinking seriously, never letting it weigh on me,
that *grave* might mean "grave." I told about my new son, my
great joy, my likeness and namesake (*Gonzalo will probably
never have children* I kept thinking). I wrote about how he was
almost walking: standing holding on to furniture and letting
go, standing upright for a few seconds before he fell (*Gonzalo
hasn't walked since he was fifteen* I kept thinking). I ran through
scriptures of put your faith in the Lord, stories of insurmountable difficulties surmounted, healings and feedings and write
back soon. I don't know if he ever saw the letter.

He died anyway.

Ordinary people have the ability not to think about things
they do not want to think about. . . . But there are some
without this ability to stop themselves from thinking, who
think all the more for being forbidden to do so.

PASCAL *Pensées*

Things I don't want to think about: cruelty, disaster, the friends
I've lost, my irrecoverable childhood, irrationality, irreducible
irrefragable irrefutable truth, fate, destiny, good fortune, infinity, pi, e, what's outside the universe, what's before the beginning, what's smaller than a quark, chaos, entropy, unmaking,
what is art and what is pornography, raped children, broken
children, battered children, the irreversible cycles of violence
and hate and pain and anger and darkness, Abraham in the
land of Moriah, three days' journey, lying to his servants, laying the wood upon his son, fire in his hand with his knife, *My
father*, Here am I, my son, *Where is the lamb?*

In making [supplication] one liberates a certain amount
of energy in oneself by a violence which serves to

degrade more energy. Compensation as in thermo-dynamics; a vicious cycle from which one can be delivered only from on high.

SIMONE WEIL *Gravity and Grace*

Isaac was delivered; Abraham was delivered, from on high. Of the many reasons explanations excuses I have heard, one sticks in my mind: God wanted, it is said, one earthly father to know his pain, what it was like to sacrifice his only son.

One time above all others I felt the great divide between theory and practice, was closest and the situation heaviest: when my son was under knife and morphine and screaming ceaselessly. He was born with a fused sagittal suture, a knob of bone at the base of his skull. No choice but to operate, this is standard procedure, nothing dangerous, we have blood on hand but rarely have to use it, he will have a zigzag scar from ear to ear, that's so his hair will mostly cover it, most kids never need a second operation, we cut away the bone front to back a strip about two inches wide, the body at his age replenishes the lost bone and lets his head grow normally, otherwise he could be brain damaged, the best time to do this is at two months. We took a rational look at the situation and made the clear decision.

The anesthesiologist, a wrinkled, sterilized man, comes to take him. *Into your hands I commend my son.* We wait impatiently, fidgeting, silent, staring at the pastel paintings on the walls, the families of the other children, the inane soap opera on the television in the corner, the half-eaten trays of food, the finger-painted magic-markered water-colored crayoned tigers and islands and bicycles and houses with V-birds and a circle-sun framed in the hallways.

The phone rings intermittently, and eventually we are cleared to see our son. They wheel him into his room, a writhing screaming tangle of wires and tubes lost propped by pillows red in the middle of a stark white stretcher big enough for adults.

I would write about the distressing pain, the helplessness, the impotence, the rage, the prayers, the fasting, the priesthood blessings, the ineffectuality of all I or my wife or medicine could do as my son screamed, two months old with his head sliced in two a strip of skull removed blood-soaked iodine-soaked bandages and butterfly strips and jagged uneven black stitches holding him together as his hands contorted and could not hold my finger could not be still shaking trembling tired of the pain the IV pulling dripping air bubbles in the hose setting alarms extra shots of morphine extra shots of ibuprofen heart-rate monitors and blood-oxygen monitors pulling away from his chest his toes nurses pulling his sock back on replacing the stickers on his chest caresses holding him tightly his mother crying tears falling to a gathering puddle on the floor beneath her hung head as he screams and writhes and screams for an entire day twenty-four hours with only short pauses to breathe *Eli Eli* never sleeping each scream a full expenditure of breath worried he won't breathe in again each time tears rage why stop this stop this *if it be thy will let this cup pass from me*

Panis Angelicus

As I was changing my daughter's diaper, I began to sing a song I had just been hearing from the children's television show *The Backyardigans*, "One Good Turn Deserves Another." It's the kind of song that repeats a line several times in a row, with slight variations in the last iteration, so that kept me going for maybe half a minute, but then I was out of lyrics and out of earshot, so I did my amateur's scat version of the melody — "Hubbaty, bobbity, boobity, beebity . . ." — and had, of a sudden, that revelation that comes to us all: *I have become my father.*

I don't consider this a bad thing. I have been consciously aiming at becoming some version of my father since I can remember. He is tall (I am taller), handsome (my wife thinks I am handsomer), intelligent (he thinks that I am more intelligent, but I don't know), strong (not to be morbid, but I expect never to beat him at arm wrestling until he is in his coffin; one afternoon, he arrived home as my brother and I were competing at pushing our car up the street; I had done it in about 1:19, David in 1:08; we prevailed upon Dad to give it a go; reluctantly, he agreed, then proceeded to muscle the car from stop sign to mailbox in 28 seconds as we cracked up laughing). He sings mellifluously, has probing thoughts about life, is kind and actively engaged in good causes. We like the same books and movies; we think similar thoughts about the state of the world and the state of our souls. Ever since I was a young man, my voice has sounded almost exactly like his; my two brothers also have this voice, which led to many minor confusions on the telephone when we all lived at home. My shoulders are unreasonably narrow for my six-foot-five frame, just like his; we both wear size 13 shoes. There are times that I, like him, stare intensely into nothing as I chew my food. There is practically nothing about my father that I don't like and want to emulate. There are a few differences, I suppose — he has a moustache and I do not, and his hair is thick and dark, though graying (mine is darkening from blonde, thinning, and graying) — but these are superficial (and could I trade my hair for his, I would do it).

But perhaps, or certainly at times, I had hoped to avoid my father's silliness. For instance, he carries on his own father's "koopertackers" style of talking to babies, a kind of gibberished gobbledygook with excitable eyebrows and melodramatic inflection. This was what I was doing, I realized, as I sang to my daughter: koopertackering. It felt good to have a name for it. She seemed to enjoy it, too.

If my father got his nonsense-talk from his father, he got his singing from his mother, from whom he and I both have inherited our ability to carry a tune, perhaps to harmonize a bit. I know almost nothing about her, but I will try to tell you a few things about my grandmother off the top of my head, to begin with:

Her name was Gladys Adele, née Vander Heyden, near the youngest of ten children of a well-to-do Dutch immigrant in Milwaukee. (John Vander Heyden owned a substantial construction supplies company, though the Depression hit hard, and he left the business to his sons with nary a cent for his daughters.) Not long after she got married, when my grandfather was fighting in France, she lived with her parents, along with her sister Marge, whose husband was also in the war, and the women gave birth to children within two months of each other. First was Marge's daughter, Diane, then my father, Patrick II, on Christmas Eve 1943. My grandfather returned from Europe when my father was two. He and my grandmother had three more children, Tom, Jeff, and Lynne, in the next decade or so, and my grandmother lived a typical life, unworthy of note in the histories and biographies, singing while she did the dishes, attending Mass faithfully, perhaps feeling a bit melancholy from time to time, until she died in 1968 from cancer. She was fifty.

I know her only in pictures and stories, or sayings short of stories, characteristics and lists, hints and reminisces, claims from one of her children to another that such-and-such is "just like Mom." I know she made wonderful pies. She seemed never to get angry at my father's shenanigans. The most common saying about her is that she had a beautiful voice. Her voice was "perfect." "She could harmonize with any song," picking out "third or fourth parts, to avoid clashing with the performers' harmonies." She had only good qualities now. Death, as we know, is a kind of expiation. The deceased leaves behind only her benevolences.

She is frozen, too, in a smattering of scattered still images that span from her twenty-third year to her fortieth, more or less, I would guess. I know her in eleven infinitesimal, imperceptible gatherings of light. This light once reflected from her, sped through a pinhole, left its mark on an emulsion. My light today reflects off that chiaroscuro to give me miniatures of my grandmother. I can hide her under my thumb. I have a photograph of her in a white dress and white shoes, off balance, pulled tight into my grandfather's embrace. In another she wears a dark suit-dress on a brick walkway at a plaza; she bends over, hands outstretched, behind my toddling father. Is she letting him go or trying to catch him? In another she sits in a metal outdoor chair on a porch, her head back, eyes shut, mouth wide, laughing. From out of the frame a hand holds both of her wrists. Then she is on base between my grandfather in uniform and a shorter friend whom nobody I know knows. In later years, she stands beside the television, in front of the fireplace and the wood paneling, above her two oldest sons in their pajamas, beside her husband who smiles into the distance past her; her eyes are downcast, her mouth pursed. Younger again, she stands beside a car with my father, my grandfather, others; she holds her right-hand fingers in a circle, index-to-thumb; her smile is for the camera, not for joy. Then she is sitting at the corner of a brick house, squinting in the sun, her hair cut short and winged on the sides; she and the chair and a branch from photo-left cast long shadows; her dress is white flowers, around her neck a triple strand of pearls, a smile that cannot be faked. She is happy.

Here she is bottom middle, hands clasped with my grandfather on her left, but she leans into, seems to support her weight on his younger brother, Jim, with his T-shirt and cocked smile and burned-down cigarette. The women form a kind of cross with mother Frances on our left, her eldest, Katherine, bent over in the middle, hanging pearls above my grandmother's head. Above is Helen, the youngest, head tilted toward her parents, right hand on Katherine's left shoulder. Sister Grace, second-youngest daughter, fills out her habit on our right hand; she smiles uneasily, as if her vows have cost her her family. My great-grandfather Daniel, top-left, turns his head away but shifts his eyes toward the camera, smiling

proudly. There is no wedding ring on my grandfather's left hand; another picture with this same tan-stuccoed house as backdrop, and Katherine and Jim wearing these same clothes, shows my grandfather in his khaki uniform, so I imagine that this picture was taken in 1941, before my grandparents were married. Perhaps he has just been called up, or he is home on leave, making wedding plans. See my grandmother with her breezeblown hair, her polka-dotted dress flowing, her eyes turned dreamily upward, her cheeks pinched in the biggest, least rehearsed smile on the page. There are leaves peeking in from the fringes, but half of the picture is unmitigated wall and windows.

As I look over the photographs I realize that in a very real way I believe that the past happened in black and white, light and shadow.

If I delved deeper, I could likely recall more of the stories I have heard about her, but I promise that in the course of writing this essay, I will find out other things. I've been wanting to know anyway, and it's really a shame that a grown man knows so little about a woman who is so much a part of him. This will take some time, but you will not have to wait long. I will compress my research into an ellipsis. Still, if you're in the mood for a sandwich or need to take care of some business in the bathroom, now would be a good time . . .

First of all, my memory had added drama to the story of my great-grandfather Vander Heyden's construction business. He had founded the company *after* the Great Depression, my father tells me, and when he died, his will stipulated that the business be sold and the profits distributed evenly among his ten children. My grandmother had already passed away by this time, so her tenth was divided among her four children. My father got about $10,000, meaning that the company had sold for only $400,000, a pitiable price, unless, as my father suspects, the uncles who had been managing the business ran it dry before the sale. This may be where I got the idea that the daughters didn't get any inheritance.

In any case, Gladys Madden was a simple woman who didn't need much, but because my grandfather was constantly changing jobs, working out of town during the week as a salesman, the family had lean years and fat years. Really, says my father, she just wanted some stability, and maybe to present a good image to the world. Her brothers, who were all quite well off, gave her grief through the years for marrying Pat Madden, "the dreamer."

I was also wrong to say that she never got angry. When my father read that, he said "Whoa! Yes she did! She got very angry all the time; I think she had a lot of trouble dealing with her mischievous sons." She had three boys before my aunt Lynne was born, thirteen years after my father, and she seems to have just wanted her children to be good, to reflect well on her. I want the same thing of my own children, and I tell them as much. "I'm responsible to see that you turn out to be a good person," I tell my son, and he nods his head, but within minutes he's kicking his sister again. I say "tell," but often it's "yell," and my words aren't usually so crafted for an audience.

When my uncle Tom brought home a wounded crow, which they named Pancho, and which they kept as a pet until a neighborhood bully shot it, my grandmother helped the boys figure out what kind of food to feed it. She was held in high esteem by neighbors and relatives, could sit down with them and chat or dispense advice with calm, but when it came to her own children, she was sometimes harsh. Once my father and Tom were racing to make their beds. To get the advantage, Tom pulled out a corner of his brother's sheets. My father ruffled two corners. Tom threw a pillow. Dad yanked a blanket. Back and forth it escalated until each had completely dismantled the other's bed and dragged it outside and they stood panting in the backyard surrounded by mattresses, linens, and bed frames. The saving grace, the call to reunite, and the cause for their laughter, which echoes today every time they tell the tale, was the realization "Mom'll be home soon!"

One summer, with my grandfather and the younger kids away in Colorado for a family reunion, my father and grandmother worked opposing shifts, he loading trucks at night at the Canada Dry bottler, and she working days as a secretary at the Perfex Corporation. He was seventeen, with cooler things to do than stay home evenings with Mom, so they spent that summer leaving notes to each other, sharing their days and nights in a few lines of quotidian happenings and musings. "It was an intimate time," says my father. "We shared feelings mostly between the lines."

She does not exist on the Internet, but I tried anyway. A Gladys Madden once performed in an off-Broadway musical comedy, a modernization of *A Midsummer Night's Dream* called *Swingin' the Dream*. The cast included Louis Armstrong as Pyramus, and the music was written by the likes of Count Basie, Benny Goodman, W. C. Handy, "Fats" Waller (as well as Felix Mendelssohn, who, I have just learned, wrote the "Wedding March" [trying to recall its melody, all I can hear in my head is the "Imperial Theme" from *Star Wars*]). The play ran at the Center Theater at 6th Avenue and West 49th Street in New York. For a split second I catch my breath. Gladys Madden had the part of "singer" (among many; at least she wasn't a "jitterbugger"). My grandmother would have loved to do just this kind of thing. But the play ran for two weeks in November and December of 1939, before she married and became a Madden.

Maybe this same other Gladys Madden sang vocals in Coleman Hawkins's Big Band around the same time. There are no Gladys Vander Heydens to speak of.

I have said that I knew her only in pictures and stories, but recently I have known her voice. When I was growing up, I often heard my father speak of his mother's brief career singing on the radio, which she gave up to raise her children. When he was a child, he rarely heard his mother sing on cue, at others' requests, but, he says, "when she was alone or nearly alone, simply performing chores, she would sing with a voice as clear and beautiful as any I have ever heard." He talked reverentially of a 78-RPM record that she and her sister-in-law Helen made sometime during the war. Helen sang alto harmony to my grandmother's soprano melody. Although the family listened to it all the time, nobody my father knew had a copy of that record today.

His uncle Jim did. I found this out by asking around, talking and e-mailing with relatives I had never met, and when I traveled to Utah from Ohio one summer, I stayed in Colorado for a day with Jim's second-oldest son, John. He had retrieved the record ahead of time, and we left the house early in search of a record player to play it on. The turntables at Best Buy were expensive; the device having become a sort of novelty item for nostalgics or necessary equipment for DJs, only high-end models seemed to have survived, and most of those spun only at 33 or 45 revolutions per minute. We kept open the option of buying one and returning it the next day, but John knew a Goodwill store that might have some used record players, so on we went. They did: an old suitcase-style, built-in-speaker model, covered in ripped burlap, with a white plastic handle, stenciled with a white LITTLETON 7TH WARD on the bottom. We plugged it in at the store counter to see if it worked. It did.

John forked over twelve bucks, despite my offers to pay.

The whole operation was very low tech, but the record was so scratched and worn that it didn't matter much. We set up the record player next to John's computer, hit *record* on the Sound Recorder program, and kept quiet. From long ago those graven vibrations brought my grandmother to me:

> Panis Angelicus
> Fit Panis hominum
> Dat Panis coelicus
> Figuris terminum
> O res mirabilis!
> Manducat Dominum
> Pauper, servus et humilis
> Te, trina Deitus
> Unaque, poscimus
> Sic nos Tu visita
> Sicut Te colimus
> Per Tuas semitas
> Dic nos quo tendimus
> Ad lucem quam inhabitas.

I held my breath, closed my eyes. The air was gritty with scratches and pops, but against this backdrop Gladys Madden sang again, with faith and power, an unwavering soprano accompanied by organ, in harmony with Helen's contralto. Within minutes we had an electronic reproduction and were burning CDs as we played the song over and over again.

That evening Uncle Jim, Aunt Rita, and their children Guy, Tim, Mary, and Kathy came to John's house to visit. We gave each other summaries of our lives and told stories. Uncle Jim taught me the old silly songs that he and my grandfather used to sing, when they weren't fighting the other kids in town, and I thought again about all of the things I would like to know and do not, about the person I would like to be and am not. My children laughed with "The Old Sow" and its attendant whistles and pops. Karina laughed and learned with me how Maddens get when they get together. Aunt Rita mentioned again and again what a lovely voice Gladys had, like the voice of an angel, she said. John played the CD; everybody fell utterly silent.

In the following months, after I and Karina and our children had moved to Karina's hometown, Montevideo, Uruguay, I stole tiny pictures of bread, angels, and Jesus to create a booklet and insert. I researched the history of the hymn (written by Saint Thomas Aquinas as part of the longer "Sacris Solemniis" for Pope Urban IV for the feast of Corpus Christi), scanned photographs of my great aunt and my grandmother, took a picture of a white carnation, her favorite flower, tested all of the fonts on my computer, bought color-printer-appropriate cardstock and plain-white sticky CD labels. I made several visits to MundoColor, a small printshop across town, to explain my plans and get pricing quotes. I found Aquinas's lines online, along with several English translations.

It means "Bread of Angels," a phrase I had not heard before but which obviously refers to the Catholic belief in transub-stantiation, a word one must practice (when one is young, learning the catechism) to get it right. In the Mass, transub-stantiation is the change from bread and water into the body and blood of Christ; the signs he chose to be remembered by become their signifieds. It is a miracle. But transubstantiations happen all the time: food into muscle and blood and bone, water to vapor to snow back to water, ideas and images into words into images and ideas in another head.

With a pinch of imagination, a rudimentary understanding of Latin gleaned from a Catholic upbringing, and a vague ety-mological sense of English and Spanish, I adapted the several published translations (some literary, some literal) to bring the oratorio into English:

> The Bread of Angels
> Becomes the Bread of men;
> The Bread given from heaven
> Fulfills all prefigurations:
> O marvelous thing!
> Upon their Lord feast
> The poor, servile, and humble.
> God, three in one,
> We implore Thee:
> Grant us Thy presence
> As we worship Thee;
> Lead us in Thy paths
> Whither we strive,
> To the light wherein Thou dwellest.

It is a glory be, a humble prayer, good tidings of great joy, and petition. I sent the finished, packaged CD to New Jersey just in time for Christmas Eve, my father's birthday. He wept with joy, my mother reported.

In 1966 my father was drafted to fight in Vietnam. He spent several months in training, signing up for an extra year of service in order to attend an electronics repair program, which he hoped would delay his deployment until Nixon pulled out our troops, or would give him the expertise to keep him on base, away from the front lines. On weekends away from Fort Monmouth, New Jersey, this Wisconsin boy excursed to Cardinal Spellman's Servicemen's Club, in New York, where he fell in love with my mother, who came in from Brooklyn with her friends for sodas and ping-pong.

When he arrived in Vietnam, he was assigned to the night

shift at the Ton Son Nhut airport. The very next day his counterpart from the day shift, walking to work, was mangled by a homemade grenade thrown by a passing bicyclist. Largely, though, my father's job with the signal corps was monotonous, removed enough from the action to be uneventful, until the Tet Offensive. He does not talk much about it all, but let us listen to what he does say, in an essay he recently wrote for *Notre Dame Magazine*:

> My job in Vietnam was superfluous. Whenever the
> Army had a serious problem, it brought in civilian
> engineers. The real point of having all of us stationed
> at Saigon airport was to have a ready group of trained
> technicians to send up country to places like Hue and
> Phu Bai. Before I was sent into the real war, the Tet
> Offensive struck. We were pinned down at our Cho
> Lon quarters with little to do but drink beer and smoke
> pot. After one particularly long and stuporous night
> watching helicopter gunships fire their rockets, I went
> to bed late, only to be awakened by the company clerk.
> Something about the Red Cross wanting to talk to me.
> I staggered downstairs and put the phone to my ear.
> "Are you sitting down?" asked the voice. I sat down.
> "Your mother is very sick and has only three weeks to
> live."

The next day he strapped himself into the sidewall seat of a C130, bowed his head, and wept all the way to his darkened home. During the dreary days in the weeks before her passing, when she was confined to a chair in the living room, she once ceded to the family's requests for her to sing. She gave them "Dear Old Girl," in a voice undiminished. The choice doesn't make much sense for her to sing, as it is a man's lament for his lost wife, and likely she sang it just because she loved the melody, but in light of what happened so soon thereafter, it is hard to avoid the thought that she was singing as proxy for my grandfather, about herself. She is the "dear old girl" I think of when I read the words:

> Dear old girl, the robin sings above you
> Dear old girl, it speaks of how I love you
> The blinding tears are falling
> as I think of my lost pearl
> And my broken heart is calling
> calling for you, Dear old girl.

She died a few weeks later, in her bed, with her family by her side. My father was reassigned to a base in Chicago, then received a hardship discharge, then married my mother, finished school, had a son.

There are a lot of things you never know. Whether the back way would have been shorter. Whether you might have done better on the test had you gone to sleep at a decent hour. Whether you might be taller or more athletic had your mother not smoked when she was pregnant with you. And so I cannot say what might have become of my father had his mother not become sick, had he stayed in Vietnam. I can say that nearly 60,000 American soldiers were killed or missing in action. This is to say nothing of the nearly 230,000 allies (mostly South Vietnamese) who were also killed, nor of the millions of dead North Vietnamese and civilians of all stripes. I can say without a doubt that in the first half of 1968, one of the worst places in the world to be dressed in uniform was Vietnam. With men falling wounded at about five times the death rate, the war left one in ten American soldiers a casualty.

And so we can only speculate about the science fiction of an alternate reality where my grandmother lives and, because of this, a lull in the offensive and a reassignment up country, a night-time grenade or a hit on the barracks, my father is killed, and I am "nothing, less than nothing, and dreams. [I am] only what might have been."

Every man is an impossibility, until he is born.

RALPH WALDO EMERSON "Experience"

My cousins sing with their grandmother in the family room. She teaches them word-by-word the old standards, the chipper tunes that teach us how life is beautiful and carefree. A shadow falls as she remembers her eldest son who used to sing with her, all those years ago.

Of course, here I am, my father is at home asleep in bed next to the chipper girl who could beat him at ping-pong, and my grandmother is long gone. And what of it? That is the way it happened, unalterably, there is nothing more to say . . . unless we alter it in meaning, exert over the past our understanding. For my father, it was a sacrifice, or a ransom: her life for his. The idea is not a trifle for him, not something he spouts at dinner parties. I only learned it recently, in a brief, heavy remark in his essay:

> Why did it have to happen? The only explanation I can muster is that this simple woman of faith had to die young in order to save my life.

I am beginning to understand, to see the sequence of events, know their inevitable results. You may claim that this was not intentional. That doesn't matter. We can still say that she laid down her life that her son might live. I repeat: I don't care whether this was intentional, whether she could will her life to end. How many of our heroes set out to become martyrs? The man in the Potomac passing the dangling lifesaver to others? What did he intend? The boys carrying the old and infirm across the freezing Sweetwater time and again? They expected to live, did they not? The firefighters running headlong, head-strong *up* the stairs?

Not long before my son was to be born, or perhaps soon after, I found myself feeling the weight of responsibility, doubting my ability. I asked my father, "When did you feel ready to be a father? When did you feel capable or capacitated?" I expected a conversation from it, but his response was forth-right: "When I realized that I would give my life for you."

It was in this spirit that I found myself nodding off on the bus after a long day bustling here and there along 18 de Julio in downtown Montevideo, between the national library, the bookstores nearby on Tristan Narvaja, the headquarters of the Movimiento de Liberación Nacional, where I was talking with revolutionaries whose aim had once been to spark one of Che's "many Vietnams" right here in Uruguay. The air was beginning to chill; leaves were beginning to turn red, then fall into the gutters, to rot and wash away. It was Holy Week, before the paschal feast, and I was leaning my head against the cold glass of the bus window as we jostled through the streets of the former San Felipe y Santiago.

As we rounded the roundabout about the Legislative Pal-ace, a pallid man boarded the bus, dressed in a black suit with an open collar. There were open seats, but he stood, holding firmly to the iron rod above our heads. I thought he looked remarkably like Fred Stoller, a sallow, deadpan actor you can Google, who plays bit parts on sit-coms like *Seinfeld* and *Everybody Loves Raymond*. He looked out with a lazy eye over his disinterested audience and began to sing.

I should, perhaps, have told you before that of all the mer-chants and mendicants who ply the public transportation, I give money only to the entertainers. I don't need cheap batter-ies or plastic bandages or indestructible pantyhose. I cringe at the trite verses and sickly cute kittens on the cards placed on each passenger's lap, "without obligation," "the value of which each person may establish in his heart." My wife's brother's friend has run too many scams — claiming to be raising money for deaf children in Pando, for teenage orphans to get job training, for battered women with no place to go — for me to trust the people who board with their rehearsed speeches and lamentations. But I can afford a few pesos for the men (they are always men) who hold on only to a guitar, who play *folklore*, as it is called, keeping their feet through turns and over potholes, who regale us for a few brief moments to take us out of the stifling heat, the numbing thrum and acrid exhaust, to the open pastures and past times of a greener, fatter land and people. That, to me, is worth at least ten cents.

Thus expectant, I was promptly disillusioned as my ears were assaulted with the singer's pained croaking. His voice wavered from one tremulous pitch to another. He tried a tango, "Volver," with its

> Sentir
> que es un soplo la vida
> que veinte años no es nada
> que febril la mirada
> errante en las sombras
> te busca y te nombra.

> To feel
> that life is just a whisper
> that twenty years is nothing
> that the feverish, errant
> stare in the shadows
> searches for you, calls your name.

and Carlos Gardel removed himself to the far reaches of heaven to escape the blasphemy. Back on earth, the passengers turned to stare out the windows into the shadows. Not a coin clanked. A young woman put in her earphones. An infectious yawn rippled outward from a seat just to my right and in front of me. I tried to read by the flaccid light. W. G. Sebald's *The Emigrants*, some lines far beyond "And so they are ever returning to us, the dead." The driver picked up speed into Belvedere, past the Pilsen warehouse, the Naval Palace, the movie theater. Nobody got on or off. The lights were in our favor.

"I would like to sing another song," said our man, undaunted. "Something keeping with the spirit of the Easter season, a hymn."

Then a melody I knew, words my grandmother sang. *Panis angelicus fit Panis hominum.* Then a kind of gossamer realization that what is only gibberish for my esteemed companions means *everything* to me. Then irrefrenable silent tears, welling, spilling. Then my pockets unburdened, a whispered *gracias*, necessary to give you in Spanish because it is beyond thanks, it is grace.

As he bows out of the scene, the bard disappears under a plane tree's umbrage. I continue striving toward the light of home.

Asymptosy

Language, in relation to thought, must ever be
regarded as an asymptote.

FREDERIC W. FARRAR On the Origin of Language

UNBIDDEN WORDS

I work with words, but they seldom come to me unbidden. So
it was a surprise when, in the middle of a family camping trip
with our friends the Nielsens in Utah's Uinta Mountains (only
hours before I found myself sitting lonely in the outhouse,
then vomiting uncontrollably behind a rock), there appeared
in my head the word *asymptotic*. I wrote it down, remembering only vaguely that it was a mathematical term, something
geometrical perhaps. I suspected that it was a gift.

Days later, after my stomach had recovered, we were visiting
the Nielsens at their home. Their brother-in-law, scant weeks
away from beginning a doctoral program in math, was wearing
a T-shirt that said "Greek cows say μ." I noted its appropriateness. "My wife got it for me," he explained, "and another
one that says, 'Kiss my asymptotes.'" (Cue chorus of heavenly
host.) To essaying!

This, then, is an essay about things, like asymptotes, that are
always approaching, never arriving. I did eventually look up
the word in the dictionary, my old college calculus textbook,

online at a number of Web sites. Our reunion was cordial. I remembered him, once I got a look at him, especially in his graphical forms. He claimed to have fond memories of me, too, though the look in his eye suggested otherwise. (With so many students breezing by him in their textbooks, who can blame him for not remembering me?) *Asymptote*: from the Greek for "not falling together." The qualitative form, *asymptosy*: from "coincidence." Yes. This feels right. The asymptote is the imaginary straight line, the apparent goal of the curve, which the curve will want to but will never quite kiss. That is fine. In any case, the relationship is reciprocal: curve approaches line; line approaches curve, ever closer, never meeting. But here we are looking at the curves, so to speak, the real world, defined by complex equations, moving in thrall to some complicated syncopation, shaped and sullied by life. We are also considering words.

> Man acts as though he were the shaper and master of language, while in fact language remains the master of man.
>
> MARTIN HEIDEGGER "Building Dwelling Thinking"

HIDDEN WORDS

On the other hand, there are a handful of words that come to me only after much thought and effort. Typically, I know their first letters and some geometric or geographical traits about them (word length, ascending and descending letters). The one that begins with a *p* that means insincere and cliché: *perfunctory*. I sat here for about twenty seconds trying to think of it, even though I knew I was going for it; I search for it often. Another p-word with a very similar meaning but in a noun form: *platitude*. If I could just associate it with a *platypus*, I think my problem would be solved, but how could

I commit such slander? How about the o-word that means apparent: *ostensible*. That one I got when I was trying for *perfunctory*, because they always travel together for me. Just the other day, I couldn't find *medley* to describe a series of songs played partially and together. It came to me today on the bus. Thankfully, it came attached to my memory of searching for it; otherwise, I might not have known what *medley* was doing in my head (and I would have had to start another essay on that word [perhaps it could appear in the previous section, with a note about how essays are themselves medleys of ideas and stories]).

> The thought was already there before, somewhere or other, and only the words were missing.
>
> JOSÉ SARAMAGO *Essay on Blindness*

There are more: *privilege*, used as a verb; *euphemism* (so useful, so ornate); a few minutes ago, revising the paragraphs above: *thrall*. In order to summon it, I had to close my eyes, place my right hand over my brow and nose, try to empty my mind of distractions (which, in turn, conjured *Ghostbusters* where Dr. Ray Stantz [Dan Aykroyd] *fails* to clear his thoughts and thus chooses the source of his friends' annihilation: the Stay-Puft Marshmallow Man). After about twenty seconds of this foolishness, *thrall* showed up, apologetic, shaking out her umbrella, mumbling something about the traffic. I was happy enough to see her that I blew it off. Better late than never.

Or, again, just now (the essay is written in the eternal now), I couldn't find the word *endorsement* for almost a minute. I had to think of Michael Jordan doing Hanes underwear commercials, which got me to *spokesperson*, which wasn't it, but which kept me focused enough to remember the word I was searching for a few seconds later.

Sometimes the words I can't find can become findable

through repeated use. Such is the case with *loath* as in "I am loath to call myself a writer because I haven't published any books," which I used in an essay once, or "I am loath to give further guidelines because I have no preconceived notion of what your writing should be," which I used on my syllabus for a creative writing workshop. I find, using my computer's indexed file searching capability, that I didn't use the word in my writing before a few years ago, but I've used it quite a few times recently. In any case, I no longer suffer such a pause to call up *loath* from my store. It has been promoted; it hangs very near the doorway to the mouth or the fingers. I suppose this is progress.

CONFUSED WORDS

And what of the words I constantly confuse? They are similar, cognates one might say, though their meanings are often as different as the proverbial apples and oranges. There's *erstwhile*, which means "once but no longer," and *ersatz*, which means "a cheap knockoff." There's *gambol*, a kind of playful walk, and *gangle* (a derivation from *gangly*), which might mean the same thing if anybody'd heard of it. There's *bold-faced*, which I took to be an ersatz *bald-faced* but which apparently is as legitimate (and nuancedly different) as an adjective before *lies*.

When we were young, my youngest brother, Dan, compounded the ribbing he took from me and our brother, Dave, by complaining to Mom, "they're making in front of me!" Dave, in childhood a king of confused words, was like the recent dunce in a FedEx commercial, thinking they're French benefits, it's the Leaning Tower of Pizza, etc. But the fact is, I can only remember one real example of the words he used to confuse. (So what does this say? It says: Keep a journal!) He misremembered "Texas takeoff" — which describes a one-footed jump in a volleyball attack (also called a "back slide") — as "flying cowboy." We still call it that today. We all know people like this: people who try on big words or dive into waters they're not prepared to swim in. They right-click serviceable terms, searching for something bigger-sounding in the thesaurus, then stuff new words in their mouths without checking the ingredients. They tend not to do well in my freshman composition classes (which, in turn, means they tend to rate me low on "respecting" them, and they're probably right).

I think this points to some gap between idea and word, thought and language. We know what we want to say or what we have associated with what others have said, or we know we want to appear knowledgeable through our words, but we fail, or we disconnect between desire and reality, theory and practice.

THE WITCH OF AGNESI

An example: among the many graceful curves described in the early years after Newton and Leibniz discovered the calculus we find the following:

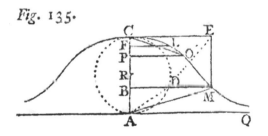

Fig. 135.

Fermat studied it around the turn of the eighteenth century, but he was to be remembered for his last theorem. Instead, the curve traces its etymology to the first mathematical book written by a woman, Maria Gaetana Agnesi's *Instituzioni analitiche ad uso della gioventù italiana*, published in 1748. This book did much to make higher order mathematics understandable to young people (thus *"ad uso della gioventù"*), paving the way for any kid with half a brain (like me!) to know the basics of the mathematics that needed the greatest minds of the seventeenth century to be discovered and developed. The curve itself is described by the intersection of parallel tangential lines at circle top and bottom with a perpendicular run through the parallel determined by a moving point on the circumference of that circle. Mathematically, its equation is:

$$y = \frac{a^3}{x^2+a^2} \quad (\text{where } a \text{ is a constant})$$

Its trailing lines (left and right in the above diagram) approach the baseline x-axis asymptotically.

Agnesi's name for this mathematical construct, *versiera*, means "that which curves," but John Colson, a Cambridge mathematician with, we may assume, only a rudimentary command of Italian and a mind that sticks with the dictionary over common sense —

> Mathematicians who are only mathematicians have exact minds, provided all things are explained to them by means of definitions and axioms; otherwise they are inaccurate and insufferable.
>
> PASCAL *Pensées*

— translated it "witch," from *l'aversiera*. Thus "the Witch of Agnesi." Or perhaps we are being too harsh on Dr. Colson. After all, he set himself to learning Italian late in life only so he could translate this exceptional book for the benefit of English youth. He died before he had time to edit the manuscript. So who's to say he wasn't having a bit of fun playing with words, as we sometimes like to do? How can we know that he wasn't planning to revise out his little joke? Perhaps he turned to that diagram on its foldout page at the back of volume one in the mid-autumn, when we remember the saints and the dead. Ah, he thought, paging through his *dizionario*, what a strange pair of near homonyms! And how appropriate for this last evening of October!

Thus we remember Maria Gaetana Agnesi, whom hearers described as speaking "like an angel"; whose two-volume treatise on integral calculus won her the queen's praise and an appointment from the pope himself to the faculty at the University of Bologna; who refused the appointment, left her mathematics behind, sold all her possessions and ran a retirement home for the poor; who dedicated her life to easing the plight of the sick and afflicted; who died at age eighty-one in the poorhouse — we associate her today with a witch, through which she has attained the majority of her nominal immortality in the histories of mathematics.

> We cannot behold without the greatest astonishment
> a person of a sex that seem so little fitted to tread the
> thorny paths of these abstract sciences, penetrate
> so deeply as she has done into all the branches of
> Algebra, both the common and the transcendental,
> or infinitesimal.
>
> JEAN ÉTIENNE MONTUCLA *Histoire des Mathématiques*

INFINITESIMALS, SUBATOMIC PARTICLES

Once again, recently, I ran into Alan, the Nielsens' brother-in-law whose T-shirt set us off on this good chase. We got to talking about this essay and others I'd written, about the incredibly vast, the approachingly infinite yet finite, the uncountable. These were familiar waters for Alan, now well into his doctoral studies. He grinned, mused inwardly, then shared with me his fascination with infinite series, how some converge to real number sums while others are unbounded, divergent, off to the races, lost and gone forever. The simplest convergent infinite series is

$$\tfrac{1}{2} + \tfrac{1}{4} + \tfrac{1}{8} + \tfrac{1}{16} + \tfrac{1}{32} + \tfrac{1}{64} + \tfrac{1}{128} + \text{etc.}$$

which, though it contains infinite terms, is equal to 1.

This makes sense, is reasonable, seems right to the mind. As each term in the series is half the one preceding it, the total grows ever more slowly with each summation. There is no point at which one cannot halve the previous term, therefore there is no point at which to stop the summation. It must continue infinitely lessening in individual terms, infinitely approaching a sum of one. Because it requires unending terms and times to reach its intended destination, the series is asymptotic to one.

> Asymptosy depends upon this, that quantity is infinitely divisible.
>
> THOMAS HOBBES *Elementa Philosophica*

The good news is that convergence is an answer to Zeno's famous dichotomy paradox, recorded and immortalized by Aristotle in his *Physics*:

> That which is in locomotion must arrive at the half-way stage before it arrives at the goal.

For Zeno, this was part of a proof that motion is an illusion. It works two ways. First, looking forward, to explain that "you can never arrive." This because if you must first reach halfway, then halfway of that first half, then halfway of that half, and so on, you have just filled your path with infinite halves and can never make a whole. Second, looking backward from the goal, "you cannot even begin." This because the whole enterprise requires an infinite number of steps, the first of which can never be determined, since any small distance can always be halved. It's a wonder a man like Zeno could get out of bed in the morning. What paralytic reasoning! (He puts me in mind of the Uruguayan writer Juan Carlos Onetti, who spent years of his waking life prone in his bed, beneath his photograph of Faulkner, smoking cigarettes, drinking wine, writing achingly melancholic stories.)

But Zeno's view of time is faulty. For him, time is a sequence of infinitesimal nows, each identical to the last. But, of course, time also has magnitude, and when a sequence of points is halved or otherwise decreased in distance, the time to traverse them decreases. Thus we may actually get there from here, which we already knew, though as we're walking, halving those halves, perhaps we may allow our minds to wonder as we wander.

> When we attend to the infinite divisibility of matter, when we pursue animal life into these excessively small, and yet organized beings, that escape the nicest inquisition of the sense; when we push our discoveries yet downward, and consider those creatures so many degrees yet smaller, and the still diminishing scale of existence, in tracing which the imagination is lost as well as the sense; we become amazed and confounded at the wonders of minuteness; nor can we distinguish in its effects this extreme of littleness from the vast itself. For division must be infinite as well as addition; because the idea of a perfect unity can no more be arrived at, than that of a complete whole.
>
> EDMUND BURKE "Vastness"

So much for Democritus's theory of the atom (from the Greek "uncuttable"). Even Golden Age Islamic natural philosophers posited the divisibility of an "atom," but when J. J.

Thomson discovered electrons in 1897 by applying an electrical field to a cathode-ray tube, the deal was sealed: atoms were more than billiard-balls; they were charged and changing. The particles Thomson posited he called *corpuscles*, though the name didn't stick. Thus arrived the atomic model we now learn in middle school: a nucleus formed of protons and neutrons surrounded by orbits of electrons.

But go on a few years, to high school or college, and you'll learn different models, more mysterious metaphors for what's going on down there in the bases of everything. The story becomes mathematical soon enough, descriptions that diverge from what we see and know about us, to questions of probabilities, incomprehensible travels and leaps across forbidden energy states. It's all abuzz in the tiny insides of things, so that if you think on it too long, you might begin to wonder that we hold together at all, that anything ever happens or exists.

Beneath the proton and neutron, there are quarks, named by Murray Gell-Mann after this line, sung by seagulls, from James Joyce's *Finnegans Wake*:

> Three quarks for Muster Mark!
> Sure he hasn't got much of a bark
> And sure any he has it's all beside the mark.

There were three quarks in 1964 — up, down, and strange — through the 1969 Nobel Prize for Gell-Mann, then, in the next decade, other quarks were needed and subsequently discovered, so that now we recognize three more — charm, top, and bottom.

And, of course, each quark has its nemesis "anti-quark," and some physicists posit "point-like particles" that make up the substructure of quarks (experimental results fail to find them). The front-runner name for them is *preons*, but since they're only theoretical, anybody can try to name them. Other options include *prequarks, subquarks, maons, alphons, quinks, rishons, tweedles, helons, haplons,* and *Y-particles.* I'm partial to *tweedles,* myself.

But what of the electron? It belongs to another class of particles, family name *lepton* (from the Greek for "small, thin, delicate"), with siblings *muon* and *tau.* These exist in "weak doublets" with corresponding *neutrinos,* and at odds with, you guessed it, their anti-particles.

> On and on it went, as if, no matter how thinly you
> sliced the world, you'd keep uncovering something
> that needed a name.
> SCOTT RUSSELL SANDERS *A Private History of Awe*

So, if you wanted to understand how quarks interact within nucleons, you might run into mathematical difficulties until you posited, then proved to modern science's satisfaction, that when quarks become very close to one another, the inter-quark force weakens, thus allowing nuclear quarks to act as free, non-interacting particles. This idea, dubbed "asymptotic freedom," first surfaced in 1973, and in 2004 garnered its proponents, David Gross, Frank Wilczek, and David Politzer, the Nobel Prize for Physics.

I don't pretend to understand what this means, nor can I envision any model other than smaller-billiard-balls (zipping about), but I like the metaphor, that at the minutest levels, particles still never quite touch, that their very proximity — the infinitesimal distances between — releases them to independence.

CAVALIERI'S SKELETON

The idea of the infinitesimal has its root perhaps in Archimedes, who disbelieved the reality of such small slices but used them nevertheless (theoretically) to determine that the area enclosed in the intersection of a parabola and a straight line is four-thirds the area of a triangle of equal base and height. The equation for this proof looks like this:

$$\sum_{n=0}^{\infty} 4^{-n} = 1 + 4^{-1} + 4^{-2} + 4^{-3} + etc. = \frac{4}{3}$$

Though he may not have known that he had done it, Archimedes had discovered the basis for integral calculus, which sums infinitesimals to determine finite areas, which Maria Gaetana Agnesi translated into words that even an Italian teenager could understand.

A century before Agnesi, another Italian mathematician played with the thin concept of infinitesimals. Bonaventura Cavalieri, of the Jesuati, the "Apostolic Clerics of Saint Jerome," who considered himself a disciple of Jesus as well as of Galileo, whom he met and corresponded with, sought some method to calculate the volumes of solid forms. (Experimental methods, such as Archimedes' famous bathhouse epiphany, were not refined or theoretical enough.) Cavalieri imagined that every planar shape was made of indefinite, indivisible parallel lines, and every solid body was made up of infinitely thin, parallel cross sections. In his first attempt at explaining his discovery, *Geometria indivisibilibus continuorum nova quadam ratione promota*, Cavalieri was not sufficiently rigorous in his justifications, thus inviting the criticism of his contemporaries. Nevertheless, he knew what he was talking about. His later work *Exercitationes geometricae sex* firmed up the proofs, established his credibility, and ensured the immortality of the name *Cavalieri*.

(As Borges mentions in the last footnote to "The Library of Babel," the library itself is "useless," as it could be replaced by a single book with infinite infinitely thin pages. "In the early seventeenth century, Cavalieri said that all solid bodies are the superimposition of an infinite number of planes," he notes.)

It is worthy of comment, I think, that Cavalieri suffered from gout, a buildup of sodium urate crystals in the joints and tendons, the conjunctions of the body. Meanwhile, Montaigne suffered from kidney stones, which are also the result of a buildup of uric acid in the blood, but these crystals are deposited in the kidneys. Cavalieri sought relief in his study of mathematics, Montaigne in his essays. Said the poet Ennius:

> numquam poetor nisi podager
> ["I never write poetry unless I have the gout."]

I know enough Spanish to decipher the Italian Cavalieri ("knights"), but let's say, for the sake of the season, the middle of the fall, that I notice, too, a similarity between *cavalieri* and the Spanish *calavera*, or "skeleton." I think Borges would approve the intentional mistranslation, to marry one celibate Catholic Italian mathematician to another in this All Hallow's Eve as the winds whip the trees and children scurry to the doorsteps. In my imagination, or perhaps in my plans for next year (how easy are plans for the uncertain future), Karina and I will dress as Agnesi and Cavalieri, and no one will know unless we tell them, trace out for them the far-fetching philological paths through which we arrived at our attire. We will seem just another witch and skeleton. But you will know.

UNKNOWN WORDS

Which brings me to the strange pleasure one feels in not knowing, in persisting in ignorance. For me, for instance, I love not knowing the lyrics of Christopher Cross's song "Sailing." Here's how it sounds to me: "Sailing takes me away to where I always doo-deet-da-dee." I've tried lots of variations, but nothing English seems to fit. Another song I don't get is the theme song from *The Jeffersons* (which was sung, I found out, by Ja'net DuBois, who also starred as Willona Woods, the Evanses' neighbor, on *Good Times*, which also has a partly indecipherable theme song). The line I don't get is "Took a whole lot of hoo-ah-ehynah / just to get up that hill." I just assumed "hoo-ah-ehynah" was something like "chutzpah." If you know, please don't tell me.

One song that is no longer a mystery to me is "Summer in the City," ever since I heard John Cougar Mellencamp speak the lyrics from the podium when he introduced the Lovin' Spoonful (whose lead singer, John Sebastian, sang the *Welcome Back, Kotter* theme song) in their 2000 Rock and Roll Hall of Fame induction. (The Lovin' Spoonful is in the Hall of Fame, yet Rush, which has sold more consecutive gold and platinum albums than any band besides the Beatles, the Rolling Stones, Aerosmith, and KISS; Rush, which has stayed together *with the same lineup* for thirty-four years, whose members are officers of the Order of Canada, that country's highest civilian honor; Rush, a band that has inspired countless bands, from Living Colour to Beck, remains out in the cold while the Lovin' Spoonful, a three-hit-wonder band that lasted all of four years, has a spot in the hallowed Hall.) The lyrics I had enjoyed misunderstanding are "Come on, come on, and dance all night / Be-bop-a-dee, it'll be all right," which Mellencamp said, before I realized what was happening, before I could change the channel or cover my ears, as "Just fight the heat, it'll be all right." Fine. But the world became ever so slightly less wonderful and mysterious for me that night.

My father tells of a music store customer who asked for "One Ton of Metal." After some back-and-forth, the man sang what he meant. It was "Guantanamera." Perhaps it's the kind of mistake a number of people could make, because there it is, on the Internet, along with somewhat less satisfying versions: "Once on a meadow," "One-dollar mirror," and the downright unbelievable: "One squashed tomato," "One ton of Maalox."

My brother once received an entire (little) book derived from misheard lyrics. It was utterly disappointing. Beyond its title 'Scuse Me While I Kiss This Guy (from Jimi Hendrix's "Purple Haze") there were only a few viable mishearings: from "Every Breath You Take" by the Police, "I'm a pool hall ace" where Sting sings "How my poor heart aches"; from REM's "Orange Crush": "We are ancient Sophocles" (Michael Stipe does have a mumbly, grumbly voice) for "We are agents of the free"; and my personal favorite, from the title line of Asia's "Heat of the Moment": "We are the Mormons." I'm surprised this hasn't been reworked into a commercial. Imagine the missionary potential! Certainly it's more rousing than the majority of the hymns we sing on Sunday. The rest of the examples in the book were unbelievably bad, by which I mean contrived and, therefore, not at all funny.

Much better than the book were the ways my friends misheard certain Rush lyrics. Rush, as we have established, is the rock band with the greatest lyrical vocabulary and the highest unique-word ratio. I'm sort of making that up, but it has to be true. Anyway, Mark Walsh taught me a vocabulary word with his confusion about "Freewill":

> I will choose a bathysphere;
> I will choose free will
> ("path that's clear")

and Vin had a nice image with

> Subdivisions:
> in the basement bars,
> in their battle cars
> ("the backs of cars")

and though I know the correct lyrics, from my manic memorizations of the album sleeves, I can't help replacing "it's a part of us" with

> Nothing to explain, hippopotamus,
> to be found within a song

in "Entre nous" (my first French lesson!). I mean, who wouldn't be pleased as punch to find a hippopotamus in a song?

Or, leaving Rush for the Beatles, my sister, who in "Paper-back Writer" believed she heard "Take the back-right turn," or my brother who, seriously or not, misheard "Watch out, I might sit on you" for George Harrison's cover of "(I Got My Mind) Set on You." Or just now, as I sit here writing, my son singing "Lucy in the Sky Comes Down."

"No, Pato, it's 'with diamonds.'"

"Lucy with diamonds comes down?"

O the minutes of joy we receive from our mishearings!

THE EXPERIMENT OF PSAMMETICHUS

While fishing around for Frederic W. Farrar's *On the Origin of Language*, quoted at the beginning of the essay (from the Oxford English Dictionary entry for *asymptote*), I discovered an offhand reference to "the experiment of Psammetichus," offered without explanation to a group of anthropologists for whom this shorthand was sufficient. I, on the other hand, had to look it up. Hear ye, then, the experiment of Psammetichus, pharaoh of Egypt who, desiring to know the origins of language, the most ancient of tongues, sent two boys to be raised in the fields by a shepherd who was not to speak a word to them nor allow them to hear human speech. Thus, the pharaoh hoped, would men know their first language, when the children began to utter in the uninfluenced, unadulterated tongue.

The notion seems hopelessly naïve to us now, with our sophisticated osmotic understanding of diversity or fluid origins or living, changing tongues. But I like the idea of the search for some primal utterance, a self-springing language born of need or given as a gift from beyond, like fire, like spirit. Before all, we may readily posit a time without language. Between then and now there was experiment and improvisation, onomatopoeia and imitation. Somebody or somebodies independently or working together first spoke, signaled, explained, repeated, and this became language.

Before I tell you what language the two babes spoke, let me tell you how Montaigne's father, influenced by the idea that the Roman and Greek languages were the portal to their civilizations' great advances, raised young Michel to speak only Latin until he was six years old. The German tutor, the servants, visitors, and family were to speak to the boy (or to each other, in his presence) only in the pure tongue,

> neither [the tutor], nor [Montaigne's] mother, man nor maid, should speak anything in [his] company, but such Latin words as every one had learned only to gabble with [him].

He learned Greek as well (though not "as well" as Latin); he was awakened every morning by music; he was encouraged to set his own schedules and follow his interests,

> to educate [his] soul in all liberty and delight, without any severity or constraint.
> "Of the Education of Children"

Karina and I, working with the languages at hand, have performed a similar linguistic experiment, teaching our children both her Spanish and my English. Our reasons, doubtless like old man Montaigne's, are practical: so they can communicate with their families on either side, so they can have some linguistic advantage in the western hemisphere, where English and Spanish are the common tongues. It's working pretty well, though they tend to favor the language of the environment they're in. Nowadays, this is English, but when we lived in Uruguay, our then-youngest, Adriana, who was three, seemed to have forgotten English entirely.

So what ever happened to those two infants raised without language by the shepherd in ancient Egypt? Herodotus writes that the guardian performed his duties admirably, providing for their needs and listening intently for their first word. When one or both of the toddlers, now two years old, with outstretched arms beseeched "*bekos*," the riddle was solved. This was the Phrygian word for "bread." Thus, we knew that the Phrygians, of the Turkish peninsula, were the original people, from whose language all verbal thought arose. Lamentably, our race seems to have forgotten Phrygian almost entirely.

FACES

From up high "upon the airy stilts of abstraction":

> It is the common wonder of all men, how among so many millions of faces there should be none alike.
>
> THOMAS BROWNE *Religio Medici*

I don't think *alike* is the best word Browne could have used. We can agree that no two faces are exactly the same, as no two snowflakes are (for one thing, they're made of different stuff), but simply *alike*? We lose the utilitarian definition of that word if we bring it so close to *identical*. Better (who could doubt it) is Montaigne's temperate saying:

> If our faces were not similar, we could not distinguish man from beast; if they were not dissimilar, we could not distinguish man from man.
>
> "Of Experience"

I've been told that I look like Jeffrey Dahmer, the serial killer (this was years ago, when the story was current; lately I've noticed that Ryan Seacrest, the host of *American Idol*, also bears a certain resemblance to Dahmer). Other people have noted that I have an air of similarity to John Schneider, who played Bo Duke on the *Dukes of Hazzard* television show. I kind of think I look a little like David Pirner, who sings and plays guitar for the band Soul Asylum (even more so because Pirner used to date Winona Ryder, who looks a bit like my wife, Karina). Or, sometimes, when I stare at the mirror in the

right way, there's something to my eyes that makes me think of Russell Crowe, the actor. This is probably only minutely visible in my mirror reflection, so don't bother looking for it.

On the other hand are people I have wanted to look like, or looked like a little bit. When I was nine or so, I bought my first KISS album (*Double Platinum*) and thought the guitar-playing space guy was the coolest, so I made special note of the way my upper lip formed a sharp, two-triangled

M-shape, just like Ace Frehley's. Later, when my favorite band was Rush, I noted how my blonde hair was parted on the left, just like guitarist Alex Lifeson's. I grew my hair long, in part to accentuate the similarities. It worked. Among the nicknames my classmates gave me (such as Batman and Iron Madden) was Alex.

And that's just the famous people I've come across in American movies, television, and music (and jails!). What of the thousands of other people who might look like me? Not even race or ethnicity need be barriers (my father looks like both Alex Karras and Muhammad Ali). Already I've had a couple of friends tell me I remind them of their brothers. One guy showed me a picture, and it's true, though his brother looks a slight bit goofier. And the other guy told me the resemblance is not so much in the face as "in movement and body type. He is tall with a long back — from neck to waist. From the back when you walk, the two of you remind me of each other."

Once, just after my father caught up with his brother Tom in New York, Tom's friends shook him down, expressing their impressedness (I wasn't yet born, so I'm going to make this up):

"That was amazing," they said.

"What was?" he said.

"How you guys choreographed that whole thing."

"What?"

"How you do everything so alike. How you walk, scratch your noses, pick the food out of your teeth. You even talk alike — your voices, your phrases. It's like watching twin robots."

This was news to Tom, news to my father, news to me when something similar happened to me and my brothers at Notre Dame one weekend.

> What a prodigy it is that the drop of seed from which we are produced bears in itself the impression not only of the bodily form but of the thoughts and inclinations of our fathers!
>
> MONTAIGNE "Of the Resemblance of Children to Fathers"

For Montaigne, this consideration was born of his aforementioned discomfort with kidney stones, which had afflicted his father, too, to death. But the statement commutes over many aspects of our beings. A dozen or so years ago, callers to the Madden household could never tell which of us men answered the phone, our voices were so alike. To make matters worse, my father and I share a name. My siblings punctuated many a phone-answering with the question "my father or my brother?"

OUR LIMITS

Which raises the question: isn't it all asymptotic? On one level, does anything ever quite reach anything else? Aren't there always gaps, spaces in between? Are we not always ever approaching, never arriving? One could go mad thinking this way, and yet.

When we are young, we draw figures outlined in black, demarcating inside and out, the limits of skin and clothes and hair. But even this: where do we end? As my fingertips touch the keys below them, sending electric signals through wires to a program designed to strike a simulated page with simulated letter forms, do I lose a part of myself? Not only metaphorically but literally: are my cells shaking lose, are my electrons jumping isotopes? And what *are* my electrons but probabilities? Am I becoming the dust that swirls and floats about me invisibly until it is caught in a beam of sunlight? Am I returning to the dust —

> velvety sinter left when matter dissolves, little by little, into nothingness
>
> W. G. SEBALD *The Emigrants*

— as the scripture says I must?
We are naught more than a temporary cohesion,

> a scrap of life, cut from the infinite fabric of the universe;
> a few of the world's atoms in love with all the others.
>
> BRIAN JAY STANLEY "The Finite Experience of Infinite Life"

Well he might have said "a few of the world's atoms in love with each other," for

> it's love that holds it all together.
>
> TY TABOR "It's Love"

Yet our borders are in flux; our insides, too. We are held in by our skin, tho' we metamorphose from our head to our toes. We sneeze: millions of molecules expelled. We take a drink: millions more ingested. We sweat, cry, rub elbows, shake hands, take off our socks, laugh, blink, breathe: we are losing our selves, the periphery is adrift to perdition, the epidermis is not impenetrable, not perdurable. Though at our smallest levels we never quite touch, we are shaken, rattled, rolled in a dizzying unrest. We never step in the same river twice, but not only because the water has changed. Even from one infinitesimal moment to the next, we are not the same. Yet we endure, somehow intact.

As we slouch in our skins, balanced on the knife's edge of the present, that infinitesimal time-point, it seems a miracle we can stay there. The same model from chaos theory would have us nudged inevitably off our perch, sent careening headlong into the future, or slipping, tumbling, into the past.

But who can bear such a supposition?

JOHN WESLEY "The Means of Grace"

SOUND CHASER

When I was fourteen, my father accepted a job transfer to the Exxon refinery in Baton Rouge, Louisiana. It was the summer before I was to begin high school, and I hated the idea of moving. Because he was a kind man, my father listened to my complaints. Because he was a practical man who took seriously his duty to provide for his family, because he had never moved very high up the management ladder within the company, because Exxon struck with almost-yearly layoffs, he decided to take the job anyway. Our debates always reduced to two clichés: "Some people live where they work, others work where they live" by me, and "Bloom where you're planted" by him.

> They could not provide me with one proposition
> to which I could not construct a contrary one of
> equal force.
>
> MONTAIGNE "Of the Resemblance of Children to Fathers"

This, I imagine, was my first understanding that clichés are worthless and contradictory, that every common notion has been packaged for rebroadcasting, that language can offer sceneryless shortcuts, and does so, more often than it takes us through new climes and panoramas. If I didn't entirely realize it then, I realize it now:

The only people for me are . . . the ones who never yawn
or say a commonplace thing.

JACK KEROUAC On the Road

Yet, for me, the magic of an essay is so often tied to its
exploding of the commonplace, its deep investigation of something we overlook or think entirely mundane and unworthy
of our attention. (And, I should note, that Kerouac quote has
become a kind of cliché itself. You've likely heard it before. A
friend of mine has it on a poster.) Most of us know the extreme,
aching delicacy with which Virginia Woolf essays "The Death
of the Moth." Most of us do not know, I suspect, A. A. Milne's
affecting autumn meditation on celery and seasons and decay,
"A Word for Autumn." In each case, and in many others, the
writer descends upon something entirely commonplace, unimportant, ordinary, then makes it fly, connects to ideas that, in
the end, mean *everything*.

But Milne's seasonal timing is all wrong for me here. Instead,
I would write about a summer day, 1986, when my best friend,
Vin, came from New Jersey to my new house in Baton Rouge
for a week's vacation.

What we did during the time that Vin was in town is almost
entirely lost to me. Doubtless he would remember a bit more.
What I remember is this:

A lingering heat after the sun has set; a gentle breeze that
seems to emanate from everywhere and blow in every direction; a gentle chorus of croaking from the canal behind my
house, across the wooden fence, hidden from view under
cherry trees and willows and tall grasses. As darkness sets in,
there is music in the air from across the canal. We are shooting
hoops, H-O-R-S-E, in the driveway; Vin is winning; when I
get a chance to take a first shot, I take a layup, jumping as high
as I can, almost dunking. The music floats by, drawing us to

it, like the sirens, like the waft of pie fragrance carrying Bugs Bunny floating to it. We set the ball against the post and walk a few steps to locate the source of the serenade. It seems to be coming from just over there. We set off walking.

Even then, I connected our walk with a recent Rush song:

> The boy walks with his best friend
> Through the fields of early May
> They walk awhile in silence
> One close, one far away.
> NEIL PEART "Middletown Dreams"

It was not the particulars, not the month or the metaphor for musical dreams. It was, I think, a connection of the most basic kind: *boy* and *friend* and *walk, close* and *far*, from the Old English, one-syllable words sufficient to convey worlds.

We walked, not in silence but in a reverential awe, realizing only partially the importance of the moment (but here it is, two decades later, while so many moments that surrounded it are gone). We chatted forgetfully about the songs, imitating Lionel Richie, Cyndi Lauper. At each corner, we were sure to have found the house or the party or the backyard barbeque that shared with the airs its radio sounds. There it is. But no.

We kept walking.

How many times were we sure? Five? Ten? More? Every time but one, perhaps a mile away already, across a major street, the music seemingly no louder than it had been in my driveway. It was a backyard party with paper lamps strung between tree branches hung with Spanish moss. It was behind a high wood fence — this gathering to which we had been wooed — out of sight except for the glow from below, the sound from around the bends and ripples in space-time that have brought the scene back to me today.

Asymptosy 135

Passing time will reach as nature relays to set the scene.

JON ANDERSON "Sound Chaser"

We stood in the street, staring. The stars shone above from so far away and so long ago that their light seemed only a feeble imitation of the scene before our eyes. So satisfied, we turned, went on our way.

RAINBOW CONNECTION

I know, because of physics or because of jading, that you can't really reach the end of the rainbow, that the ephemeral scattering of light will move away from you as you move toward it until your angle is no longer right and it disappears. But I am descended in part from the Irish, and my name is Patrick, as is my son's, so one spring afternoon when we looked out back and saw a giant arc that seemed to land right in our neighbor's back yard, we took off on our bikes to find the pot o' gold, a straight shot down 700 South toward the ephemeral curve in the distance. Patrick was seven then, excited to be riding out of our neighborhood, with his dad.

Look at my son: his orange shirt with blue sleeves, his blue-jean shorts, his sinewy arms and legs, the short socks his mother buys for him, the dog-bitten gray sneakers that he keeps tied and slips on and off. Look at his long curls poking out of his helmet, catching the sun, blowing in the wind. (Remember, with this phrase, the day he asked from the back of the car, "Daddy, how many years can a mountain exist before it gets washed into the sea?" I thought he was profound then. "I don't know," I said. "That's a good question. It must be a long time." "Nope," he shot back. "The answer, my friend, is blowin' in the wind!" He was so happy to have tricked his dad.) Look at his tanned arms, imagine the cilia-like blond hairs there. This is my firstborn; I am my father's; my father was his father's. We each bear the same name, like further iterations of the same attempt at humanity, some approximation, some approach at something more.

We rode, faster then slower, and I tried to explain how light refracts from floating drops of water, separating into component colors — the ROYGBIV order of things — how the names we give to colors point at gradations, how red is not orange yet there is no dividing line, one color transforms into the next and the next infinitesimally different from the others around; and thus, see? the rainbow is over there now, because what we're seeing is conditions propitious for rainbows, each slightly different, depending on the observer. If a rainbow falls in a forest ... My son smiles from under his space-alien bicycle helmet. He seems content never to arrive at that bridge to the afterlife, that chariot of the gods or cloak of the Great Spirit (whatever we may name it, to approach it); he is okay just being near his father, riding east, doggedly pedaling.

Singing

*I am home again for Thanksgiving, at my parents' house, now
with a wife and children of my own; my father's old Vietnamese
amplifier and cassette deck and reel-to-reel are somewhere in the
attic, having been replaced by newer technology and worn down by
constant use (only the reel-to-reel still worked when it was retired);
in their relative place against the north wall of the family room in
a new entertainment unit sits a compact all-in-one sound system,
one of the few in the store with a phonograph; we haven't had
time yet to sit down and sing like we used to because he's been
off to work or somebody wants to watch a television program or
we're too tired.*

I was raised on the Beatles, the Eagles, and Steely Dan,
these three, but the greatest of these is the Beatles.

In my youth, singing was like breathing, a natural effortless
occurrence that always was and always would be. I sang with
my father in the living room mostly, picking out harmonies
with him, following his lead, venturing on my own now and
then, listening to the underlying music not with an analytical
mind, not seeking the thirds and fifths that fit well with the
given chords, but with a kind of instinctive feel, awash in the
sounds and ecstatic to meld my own voice with the voices
coming from the phonograph, with my father's voice in the
room embracing me.

Two of the gills with which our rudimentary ancestors breathed in the days when they were sea dwellers have become vocal chords.

RALPH MORSE BROWN *The Singing Voice*

Yet the comparison of singing and breathing is too melodramatic, as if to exaggerate the influence and the importance of singing. I want to rescind my overzealous claim, temper it with something more realistic. I loved singing; I am eternally grateful to my father for teaching me — not so much teaching me but inspiring me, demonstrating, singing with me so I would teach myself to sing. I could sing along with Paul McCartney or John Lennon or George Harrison or Ringo Starr before I learned to distinguish their voices. We sang often — how often I can only venture to guess, though my memory of singing is so seminal, so constant that I feel as if we were always singing, and it pains me to concede that we may have sung only intermittently. What's certain is this: our singing was never a special occasion, never the answer to "What do you want to do?"; we never had to wonder what to do, when to do it, what record to put on. Such details were superfluous to the act itself.

So I might say that in my memory of singing in my formative years, an act disconnected from time and circumstance, I am *always* with my father, we are always taking parts and playing off each other as the Beatles played off each other, the resonance lifting my spirit now as I reflect almost as much as it did then, before I realized it.

My father is an engineer and I a physicist; I inherited his mathematical ability and, because such an ability was rare, developed it because I loved logic, a rational thought process, solving a difficult problem, where there are right answers and wrong answers and no ambiguity, no difficulty in expressing reasons.

I found out later that my father had seriously considered changing his major from chemical engineering to music, this in the middle of his senior year of college. He sang second tenor in the glee club at Notre Dame. He sang at his sister's wedding, "The Wedding Song," with his brother, Uncle Jeff, and they both played guitar, and I carried my aunt's and her husband's wedding rings on a pillow in my brown velvety suit with a girl I can't remember next to me bringing flowers.

I have heard the song sung by many singers, but I always imagine it as my father and my uncle sang it that day.

Singing is sometimes an avenue to discovery, even inane discovery.

Sing the ABC song out loud. (ABCDEFG / HIJKLMNOP / QRS/ TUV / WX / Y and Z)

Now sing "Twinkle, twinkle, little star."

Do you hear it? They're the same tune.

Now try "Baa, baa, black sheep."

Wonderful.

Though I have since heard the connection between the first two songs mentioned by Telly on *Sesame Street*, I figured out this connection on my own and have been spreading the good news ever since. I have yet to meet anyone who knew it already. I have met many who didn't care, but there are also many who are fascinated by it like I am. And what of "The Itsy Bitsy Spider" and "Sweetly Sings the Donkey"? Or "He's a Jolly Good Fellow" and "The Bear Went over the Mountain"? How could we not know that these songs, a part of our culture, sung by children all over the country, share tunes with one another?

Singing unifies.

In singing, we express a shared experience. We have memorized the same words, learned songs in similar settings, held common beliefs. We become united in song even though we may have never met. The national anthem at a sporting event, the hit song performed at a concert, the theme to a favorite television program, all provide the opportunity for unity.

Elder Kalu and I, missionaries in Durazno, Uruguay, he Nigerian, I American, both former Catholics turned Mormon, both former altar boys, would sing our forsaken church's hymns as we rode our bicycles under the colorful turning leaves lining the streets. He sang in a deep, melodious baritone that resonated in his chest and was layered with an airy rasp. I sang harmony above him. "And he will raise you up on eagles' wings," we sang, and I imagined that because we sang in a language the people we passed couldn't understand, we were invisible, inaudible, somehow floating above it all, carried on our way.

Singing is both admired and scorned, encouraged and discouraged; it takes guts to sing.

Our relationship with singing is a paradoxical one. On the one hand, we love singing and heap fame and fortune on those among us who do it well or interestingly or with a tinge of some originality of voice that sets them apart. Good singing combined with good songwriting ability and a bit of savvy and lucky timing can lead to one of the most lucrative jobs in the world.

Paul McCartney, by some estimates, is the third richest man in Europe and certainly one of the richest men in the rock business. He, David Bowie, Mick Jagger, Elton John, all have amassed hundreds of millions of dollars because of their singing and business ventures. While much of their income may be from investments, and their singing would be worthless without their corresponding songwriting abilities, the seed of their fortunes was their singing. Had they not loved to sing, would they have ever bothered writing songs?

Yet we also are ashamed of our singing, or I was, when I was younger. We are nervous about public performance, our voices crack, we are silenced by shame of not singing well. When I was young, singing exuberantly at home with my father, I rejected the school music director's invitation to sing in the choir. I suppose I was partly worried that I would be called a sissy, but more than that I was simply too self-conscious to sing in public where others could hear me and make fun of me.

One time I and two other motorists, whom I could see in my rearview mirror, were singing the same song at the same time.
    In public, for me, sometimes includes in my car in traffic singing along with the radio, even with the windows rolled up so no one can hear me (I think), because others can see my unnatural movements, the emotion on my face as I sustain a long note or run down a scale. So I sometimes feel a tinge of shame when I catch a fellow motorist ecstatically air drumming and carefree. Still other times I feel inspired, and, frankly, I'm getting over my fear. But one day, when I was a new driver, just seventeen, and driving to the mall, I was singing self-consciously along with "Every Breath You Take" by the Police. I was watching people in my rearview mirror, watching to see if they were watching me singing, and I noticed, one after another, a man and then a woman both mouthing the same words I was — "How my poor heart aches with every breath you take" — and I felt that strange liberation, a kind of kinship and approval.

Singing is at once natural and unnatural.
    During my senior year at Notre Dame I lived near a lot of friends who were also seniors. One day I was hanging out with them in their "party room," and — it seems to happen spontaneously in my memory, either that or it was my idea — we

decided to sing instead of talking, just like a musical. Perhaps we were talking about the silliness of musicals, breaking out into song as if it were spontaneous, perhaps we were wondering at our own willingness to suspend disbelief. In any case, we wanted to try it, make a real-life musical. Granted the idea was not entirely unique — at least I have seen it done since on *The Simpsons* — but it was one of those college senior things. I think it may have been during finals week.

It ended up being somewhat entertaining, but not really. Most utterances were sung either to standard melodies (stuff like the aforementioned "Twinkle Twinkle Little Star" or "Happy Birthday") or random cacophonies. But it was fun, and it was memorable, if only because we did it. It was also taxing, hard to keep a good melody. And rhyming? Forget about it.

Cantar es disparar contra el olvido.
[To sing is to fight against forgetting.]
JOAQUIN SABINA "Todavía una canción de amor"

As a direct result of singing so often with my father when I was young, and possibly due to a proclivity for remembering words accompanied by music, my brain has a large portion of its memory space devoted to song lyrics. I am not saying I ever found it useful to rely on made-up songs to keep track of all fifty states and their capitals or all the prepositions, but real rock and roll songs, those are with me. For instance, whenever I see a white car or even more when I hear somebody say "white car," I hear the obscure Yes song "White Car," which is supposedly about Gary Numan (one-hit-wonder singer of the '80s pop song "Cars"), in which a man in a white car "move[s] like a ghost on the skyline."

And that's only one example of many. Lyrics are popping in my head all the time triggered by something I hear or read.

(Side note: *sing* as a noun can mean the noise made by a bullet as it flies through the air, which is interesting because my translation above is slightly altered to avoid a strange-sounding sentence, but *disparar* actually means "to shoot at.")

Sing is a purely Viking word, with variants in Old English, Old Frisian, Old Norse, Old Swiss, Old High German, and Old Dutch, but none in Latin or any Romance language.

Everybody can sing, and probably does sing, even if it's when nobody else is listening.

Sing, sing a song.

KERMIT THE FROG

My father, reading over my shoulder, says that Karen Carpenter sang the sing-a-song song before Kermit the Frog, but I always hear it in Kermit's voice. I think the simple message of the song, directed at children when it comes from *Sesame Street*, is a good one. I can't remember when I became self-conscious about my singing. I know that even when I was shy in school, I was singing at home. I wonder if our shame of singing is something like the shame we feel of our bodies if we're not in model shape, an environmental conditioning of our timidities.

We may sing even to our own detriment.

One Friday just before noon I was driving from Salt Lake City to Brigham Young University in Provo to read an essay of mine as part of that week's creative reading series. Normally, established authors and poets read, but once a semester the director asked three graduate students to do short readings of their work. This was my turn.

I had been on an editing internship in Salt Lake City for

the whole semester, so I had to leave work early and drive for almost an hour to get back to school. On the way I blared my radio and sang along with Aerosmith's "Dream On," Def Leppard's "Photograph," Led Zeppelin's "Stairway to Heaven," Rush's "Tom Sawyer," so many songs I can't remember. I probably shouldn't have been listening to the hard rock station because by the time I got to Provo, my voice was shot. I gave my reading anyway, with a brief excuse, a quick note to the appropriateness of my condition given the Jimmy Page reference in my essay, and a little help from the microphone.

Different peoples understand singing differently; the way we sing in the West is quite different from the way people do it elsewhere.

Richard Feynman, Nobel-prize-winning physicist who worked on the Manhattan Project and discovered the O-ring failure that caused the Space Shuttle Challenger's explosion, introduced me (not personally, through his writings) to the throat singers of Tannu Tuva, which I have since heard on National Public Radio. These are men who, by strictly controlling the passage of air through their vocal chords, can produce up to five distinct tones simultaneously. Their singing is strangely haunting, something like a didgeridoo, not much at all like the singing we're used to, so different, in fact, that it's hard to imagine the sound being produced by a human voice.

When God laid the foundations of the world, the morning stars sang.

Imagine this: Job, who has lost everything, his herds, his grains, his children, his home, his wife's love, who has been outcast precisely because he refuses to curse God for his misfortune, has misspoken out of ignorance. God, angry, vengeful, reproaches Job, challenging:

Where wast thou when I laid the foundations of the earth? declare if thou hast understanding ... Whereupon are the foundations thereof fastened? or who laid the cornerstone thereof; When the morning stars sang together, and all the sons of God shouted for joy?

Job 38:4, 6–7

Here is singing interlaced with the great mysteries, the foundation of the world, the unanswerables that God only knows. Here is singing primordial and poetic.

Singing can heal.

Every Wednesday morning my son has therapy for his uncontrollable behavior. His doctor suspects that he has Attention Deficiency Hyperactivity Disorder, but he's too young to bear that label, and we want to exhaust every means of correctional treatment before attempting to regulate him with drugs. We take him to a local school for handicapped children, mostly mentally retarded kids whose abnormalities are visible on their faces and in their contortions or wheelchairs or braces. When he gets loose, Patrick runs around like a maniac, ducking and hiding behind wheelchairs, tearing through groups of kids eating or reading or playing with clay. By the time we're done with his therapy, done swimming, and ready to go home, usually around 9:30, the kids in the school are circling the outer edges of the gym along with their teachers. From the middle of the room a stereo plays popular children's songs, and teachers and students dance their slow dance, pacing or rolling in continuous circles. Some few of them, those whose voices and minds can so combine, sing along, and their teachers encourage them. I stand by waiting, and I reflect on the gift of song. I think, somehow singing can make these children whole.

Even my mother, who can't *sing, can sing.*

I sometimes make myself believe that a good singing voice is a gift, something you're born with that training can improve but cannot create. Yet I have proof of the contrary: that training, or practice, can develop one's ear, refine one's sense of harmony. My mother, for instance, is what you'd call tone deaf. She sings along with her 1950s bee-bop rock, and sometimes she hits the right notes, but by and large her voice and the voice on the radio are in disagreement. She grew up an only child in a home with nonsinging parents. My younger brother, five years my junior, grew up possibly with more of my mother's singing genes than I did, but also in a time when my father no longer spent so much time singing along with his records. David also was tone deaf, for a time, and we made fun of his singing off key. But in recent years, he has learned to sing. I asked him how he did it and he told me, "One day I just realized that you can't just sing any old note and expect to be in tune. So I started really paying attention, studying what notes they were singing, and I forced myself to copy them."

By way of contrast, I was shocked by the dissonance of the hymns in the first church meeting I attended as a missionary in Uruguay. The congregation was made up mostly of working-class folk whose luxury time was spent sipping *maté*, a scalding-hot herbal tea, and watching television. They had, I could suppose, very little practice in singing, much less with Mormon hymns they had never heard before their conversions, and without the guidance of a piano accompaniment, they were hopeless. I grew, however, to feel a certain fondness for their brand of singing. Everybody sang unselfconsciously, many people at a full shout, and even now when I reflect I feel somewhat ashamed of my elitist ear.

Singing can make you laugh.

Sister Vecchio, the chorister in the Danubio Branch of the Mormon Church in Montevideo, leads the hymns each Sunday without the benefit of a piano. She knows the melodies, however, and she does a good job of maintaining an even tempo and steady pitch. Where she has problems is when she encounters a hymn whose subject matter seems very much like another hymn's. She doesn't actually read music, so several times she has sung one hymn's words to the music of another. Amazingly, sometimes the words fit right in and the congregation is none the wiser, but more often than not, the mix-up leaves syllables either shortened or hanging at the end of a line of music, the small congregation bemused and eyeshifty, my missionary companion and I barely stifling an uproarious gutlaugh.

Singing is exercise.

In Durazno, Uruguay, I served among two Mormon congregations that met in the same building, one at nine o'clock and one at eleven. Elder Kalu and I attended both wards' sacrament meetings. During the earlier meeting the young girl who led the music (again without a piano to guide her) began each song much too low. When the line of music tried to go lower, most of us couldn't do it, and we were left open-mouthed like fish, trying to resonate. At the next meeting, the chorister began each song too high, and with each small rise in note, the air was filled with shrilling falsettos or octave-dropping bassos.

Singing is the best way, short of sleeping (which you can't do when you're driving) to pass the time on long road trips; it helps keep you awake, too.

At the end of summer 1999, my father and I drove a Ryder moving truck east from Utah to Ohio. The truck was packed with my family's things, but because my wife was pregnant and my son was small and ill-disposed to such a long journey, my father volunteered to drive the truck with me while my mother flew back to New Jersey with my wife and son to wait for us after we'd unloaded the boxes and furniture in Ohio. That's the explanation. Here's what happened and how it relates to singing.

The truck had air conditioning but no radio. We are like minds, my father and I, but there's only so much you can talk about on a four-day cross-country trip, only so many car games the adult mind can take, and only one billboard announcing Vasectomy Reversal Surgery in Houston, Texas (it's in Missouri on Interstate 70) to laugh about, and even that laugh lasts only a few minutes, so we spent much of our time singing.

Round songs are perhaps the best songs to sing without any guitar and drums as back up, and so we sang "Row, Row, Row Your Boat," "Sweetly Sings the Donkey," and the three-part combination of:

> One lollipop, two lollipop, three lollipop, four lollipop, five lollipop, six lollipop, seven lolli lollipop.
> Don't put your junk in my back yard, my back yard, my back yard. Don't put your junk in my back yard, my back yard's full.
> Fish and chips and vinegar, vinegar, vinegar. Fish and chips and vinegar, pepper pepper pepper salt.

We also sang a lot of "Take Me Out to the Ball Game," varying the wording by cutting off progressively one, then two, then three (and so on) syllables from the beginning of the song but carrying the same tune so that the ending ("at the old ball game") would end on different, unresolved notes. It was fun. We tried the same technique with other songs (especially difficult with the "One lollipop" song, but especially good results also) and had a hard time singing through our laughter. Are you lost? Here's what I mean: you sing the same notes as you normally would, but you begin one or more syllables into the lyrics. "Take me out to the ball game" would be "Me out to the ball game, take" sung to the same tune as the original. Try it. It leads to some humorous misaccentings of words (iambs into trochees and vice versa [with the mention of the word iamb, my mind is thrown into "Sex Type Thing" by Stone Temple Pilots: "I am, I am, I am"]), and mostly, the strange unfulfillment of your end-of-line musical expectations. There's something pleasurable about it.

All that was wonderfully fun, but by far the best singing invention we made on that maddening trip was the extension ad nauseam of Shirley Ellis's "The Name Game" song from the 1960s. You can try it with any word, like the song says, but the most fun are the words with the most syllables. (The best word to sing there [we proved it] is *Alabama*:

Alabama, Alabama, bo balabama, banana fana, fo falabama, fee fi, mo malabama. Alabama!)

And when they had sung an hymn, they went out into the mount of Olives.
Matthew 26:30; Mark 14:26

Singing: the last act of Jesus with all his apostles before his death. Singing as sorrow, farewell. Singing as comfort. I want to know the hymn they sang.

Singing voice is like a fingerprint: even though every new singer you hear on the radio may sound exactly like Eddie Vedder from Pearl Jam, each voice is actually unique.

Female vocal chords, five-twelfths of an inch long on average, vibrate between 150 and 850 times per second, according to Robert Morse Brown. This is roughly twice as fast as male vocal chords (except those of Tiny Tim and a slew of 1980s hair-metal-band singers), which are, on average, seven-twelfths of an inch long. Vocal chord vibration is controlled by nerves and muscles in the throat, air bellowed through the chords by the lungs, all of which are controlled, ultimately, by a singer's brain.

Singing can relieve stress.

The two years I spent in Uruguay as a missionary were often stressful. On too-hot afternoons, when there was nothing better to do, Elder Gray and I would sometimes break into Metallica's eponymous "black album," recasting "Holier Than Thou," "The Unforgiven," or "Wherever I May Roam" (all spritely missionary songs) in operatic strains or country twang.

I am growing less afraid of singing in public.

We had just read "Los Angeles Notebook" by Joan Didion for class. A student raised her hand and said, "You know it's really pronounced Santana winds, not Santa Ana."

"Okay," I said. "But I know in the Steely Dan song they say 'Santa Ana,' two words."

"Steely who?" said a student.

"Steely Dan. Don't ask me what it means." I sang the line I'd just mentioned, "Here come those Santa Ana winds again."

"What other songs do they sing?" asked another.

"You know," I sang, "Are you reelin' in the years?"

Nothing.

"'Rikki Don't Lose That Number'? You know, 'You don't wanna call nobody else.'"

Silence.

"You go back, Jack, and do it again / Wheel turnin' round and round."

That one they have heard, and I have just sung in front of an entire class.

Singing expresses opposition, protest.

Singing can be political, a reaction against an oppressor, a mode of communication, unification, among marginalized peoples. I am thinking of Negro Spirituals, 1960s folk-music rock and roll. I am thinking of Christianized slaves, awakened to the heinous paradox of their bondage to their lighter-skinned brethren in the faith, learning the stories of the Bible, finding a mirror of their plight in the slavery of the children of Israel in Egypt, singing, "When Israel was in Egypt's land, 'Let my people go.'" I am thinking of multicolored, swirling, long-haired, bearded, and unwashed hippies carrying signs and singing, "All we are saying is give peace a chance." We learn the words that express our concerns. We sing along.

There is miracle power in singing, as praise and prayer.

> And the multitude rose up together against them: and the magistrates rent off their clothes, and commanded to beat them. And when they had laid many stripes upon them, they cast them into prison, charging the jailor to keep them safely: Who, having received such a charge, thrust them into the inner prison, and made their feet fast in the stocks. And at midnight Paul and Silas prayed, and sang praises unto God: and the prisoners heard them. And suddenly there was a great earthquake, so that the foundations of the prison were shaken: and immediately all the doors were opened, and every one's bands were loosed.
>
> Acts 16:22–26

What is this singing that shakes foundations, brings peace in the midst of strife, this harmony of immortal spirits that, according to Milton, "Suspended Hell"? What is the power of singing? What is its meaning, its cause, its definition?

> The night they let me out I heard murmurings and distant voices and sounds of metal clanking while I walked through corridors, a guard at either side. Then the prisoners began to whistle, softly, as if blowing on the walls. The whistling grew louder and louder until one voice, every voice as one, broke into song. The song shook the walls.
>
> EDUARDO GALEANO *Days & Nights of Love & War*

Singing, for me, is an heirloom, an inheritance, a gift, that I want to share with my own children, a gift I've received from my ancestors.

My son is now going on three years old, and I have begun to train him up the way my father trained me. We sing many of the same Beatles songs I once sang with my father, mixed in with some more contemporary bands that I have picked up along my way, and although my son is still too young to figure out harmonies or memorize lyrics, he can add his voice to mine just the same.

A little over a month ago my parents came to visit. My father and I drove to Columbus to pick up my youngest brother and bring him to Athens for a semi–family reunion. All the way back we listened to America and the Eagles (one speaker was broken, and George Martin's experiments in stereo recording make listening to Beatles songs through only one speaker inadvisable), and we joked and laughed and reveled, singing in three-part harmonies that shook the air.

Now, earlier today, out of nowhere, in the kitchen, my father sang "Let's all get up and dance to a song," I joined in, "that was a hit before your mother was born." And onward and my own son, hearing a song that truly was, metamusically, a hit before his mother was born, joined his voice to his father's and his grandfather's. Three generations of Patricks, II, III, and IV, singing jubilantly a song that Patrick I, not much of a Beatles fan, once called, "pretty good," his highest compliment for the Fab Four, and I didn't think of it then, but as I write I wonder, if what we believe is true and if I might not be too unoriginal or sentimental to wonder, as many have wondered before, if we might have been joined by a fourth harmony.

Singing is always on my mind and often on my tongue, as I think through a filter of song lyrics, as I write and think thematically and fragmentedly, after my essayistic influences; of all the themes running through my life, singing is one of the most pervasive, the most constant.

Hepatitis

On Wednesday, our anniversary, our son got sick, throwing up in his bed and on the wall in the middle of the night, then again in the bucket I had placed next to him after the requisite sheet stripping and floor mopping and teeth brushing. On Thursday our daughter got sick, throwing up — or "growing up," as she calls it — with enough warning to make it to the bathroom sink. On Friday, the dog had trouble breathing and would fall suddenly, hard, thudding on the concrete path that connects the iron gate near the street with our front door.

My wife's little sister had fallen ill with hepatitis a couple of weeks earlier, one of thirty-eight children and two teachers at a school in northern Montevideo whose pipes, rumor had it, had broken somewhere outside and were mixing outgoing bathroom water with incoming drinking water. A few days after her little sister, Karina's father fell ill. Years of heavy drinking had left his liver in bad condition, and his hepatitis would confine him to his bed for four months. Karina had had hepatitis when she was a kid (the disease is common in Uruguay), and I assumed that my children and I, born in the United States, had been vaccinated against the disease. Only after Pato spent the night vomiting did I call Ohio to ask for his and his sister's vaccination records and learn that they had been inoculated against hepatitis B, but not A. That vaccine, said the nurse, was given only if parents requested it, for instance if they were traveling to South America.

So Karina spent Wednesday morning at the hospital getting an appointment so she could spend the afternoon at the hospital getting the children's papers straight (they are Uruguayan citizens, and therefore qualify for public health care) so they could spend the evening at the hospital getting the blood test that would confirm the bad news that Pato had hepatitis. Because Adi was then skittish and happy, they wouldn't test her. I spent the day researching hepatitis on the Internet to channel my nervous energy to some kind of solution. I fretted, feeling I had left my children unprotected, had put too much faith in the force field granted by science and medicine in the First World. What I found was both interesting and frustrating. There was a lot of information about contracting the disease, or avoiding it, through vaccinations and precautions, but almost nothing about treating it. From the Centers for Disease Control's site I learned that hepatitis A is a virus that attacks the liver, often leaving the infected person jaundiced, tired, nauseated, without an appetite, with diarrhea, with vomiting, with fever, which is not very different from having the flu, except that it lasts longer, usually about a month. Some people never show any symptoms, and their bodies fight the virus quietly, behind the scenes, with no glory or recompense. Hepatitis A has no long-term effects, and once you've had it you can't get it again. Uruguayans are convinced that once you've had hepatitis A, you can never donate blood or organs, but nowadays, this is not true.

In the United States, you're most likely to find hepatitis A in the West and Southwest, where many counties reported more than twenty cases per 100,000 people during the decade of 1987–97. There were far fewer reported cases in the East, with West Virginia and South Carolina leading all states in hepatitis A safety (fewer than five cases in any given county). There are between 125,000 and 200,000 cases of hepatitis A in the United States each year. Internationally, Uruguay is one of the countries with the highest danger of hepatitis A infection, along with basically all of Africa, South Asia, Central America, Paraguay, Bolivia, Ecuador, and Greenland. I was curious that Greenland would be a high-risk country for hepatitis, especially being situated in the Arctic, in the neighborhood of Iceland and Canada, which both have very low risk. I learned that Greenland is a home-ruled province of Denmark, having achieved its semiautonomy only in 1979 after centuries of Nordic rule (first Norway, then a combined Norway and Denmark, then Denmark). It's true that the name Greenland (Kalaallit Nunaat in Greenlandic and Grønland in Danish) was a Viking marketing device to get settlers there in the centuries after Erik the Red discovered it, and that the island (the largest island in the world) is mostly buried under ice and only green on the coasts during summer. I'm always happy to find out that some crazy rumor I've heard here or there is true, because, basically, that story about Greenland's etymology always sounded too tidy, kind of suspect. I was also happy to find that Greenland's National Tourism Board owns Greenland.com instead of some parasitic cybersquatter. Nothing on Greenland.com indicates why the country has such a high incidence of hepatitis A.

On Thursday, fearing I would be next to fall, I went to the British Hospital to get a gamma globulin shot to boost my immune system's ability to fight off contagion. On the bus there, I read from José Saramago's *Blindness* — a dystopic novel about a plague of blindness, whose Portuguese title, *Ensaio Sobre a Cegueira*, translates to *Essay on Blindness*, which I like

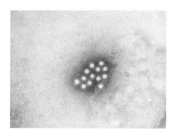

much better than the market-driven, unchallenging, purely descriptive title it ended up with — in which the aphoristic omniscient narrator invited me to "consider the circumvolutions of the human mind, where no short or direct routes exist."

Hepatitis A has maybe the worst way of spreading of any disease I've ever heard of. Clinically, it's a "fecal-oral" transmitter, which gives new meaning to the old vituperation. (*Vituperation*, I admit, is a retrofound word, from the fairly common Spanish *vituperación*, which happens to exist in English but is, I realize, not common at all. It means a malediction, a curse, an insult. I think the word *vituperation*, despite Ferdinand de Saussure's assurance that words are arbitrary signs unrelated to the things they signify, sounds like it *should* be a word that means insult or curse. Sounds like you're spitting at someone.) I had such a hard time believing that, or believing that that was the only way it could spread, that I asked Dr. Kleist, of the British Hospital, when I went in. He confirmed it. Hepatitis A spreads only from oral ingestion of feces. To me it seems like a body ought to always react with nausea and vomiting when it ingests human feces. The thought staggers the mind: if a disease like this can spread to new hosts, and they've all eaten fecal matter infected with the virus, then how often do people eat noninfected fecal matter? I don't really want to know.

Of course it's not so simple as eating the stuff. People get infected by drinking unclean water, by close contact (sharing a cup, utensils, foods) with an unwitting carrier of the disease who hasn't washed his hands after using the toilet, by eating raw or partially cooked shellfish caught in polluted waters. You can get the disease without engaging in overtly risky or unhygienic behaviors. But still. It's no wonder the disease is stigmatized. It spreads where water and people are unclean, but also where people are clean and unlucky.

Gamma globulin, I should mention, does not impart super-human powers like you might expect given its name. It simply strengthens a person's immune system to fight off infections like hepatitis, but it only works for about three months. What's good about gamma globulin is that it can be administered after you've been exposed to a disease (it works for measles and rubella as well). That's why I wanted it. Dr. Kleist explained that a product such as the one he gave me (manufactured by Bayer, which is "almost an American company," he said, I think to inspire my confidence) is made from human plasma, and the manufacturer cannot guarantee that its product will not give me some disease that it should protect me from, even AIDS. I realized that he was bound by law to explain this and get my consent before giving me the shot, and that there was probably no real chance that I'd get infected, but the information gave me a hard pause. I kept my questions and my doubts to myself, though, afraid of breaking rhythm, offending protocol, like a person who really tells you how they're doing when you ask. I had had gamma globulin shots before, and Bayer certainly wouldn't be very successful in business if its products infected or killed people. I remembered hearing that there was strong opposition to the polio vaccine when it was originally developed, that people worried that the vaccine would give them the disease, which, coincidentally, is also a fecal-oral transmitter. Even today, clerics in parts of Nigeria, which produces half of the world's new polio cases each year, are advising their people not to take the vaccine because, they say, it is actually part of a Western plot to render Islamic women infertile and curb Africa's population. Their resistance in the past has led to reinfection of children in six neighboring countries previously declared polio free. With India, Nigeria is the last bastion of the disease that once affected millions of children. In 2003 only 700 cases of the disease were reported worldwide, which is a vast improvement from 1988's 350,000 cases but a step up from 2001's 483.

Nigerian clerics are not alone in their wariness of vaccines. One in 2.4 million people inoculated with oral polio vaccine does contract the disease. Edward Hooper's 1999 book *The River* theorizes that 1950s polio vaccines developed by Dr. Hilary Koprowski, which used polio virus grown in Asian monkey kidneys, caused the current AIDS epidemic. Hooper points to the coincidence of early HIV infections and oral polio vaccinations in Central Africa, speculating that Koprowski or his associates grew some of their polio virus using tissue from chimpanzees, which carry the SIVcpz virus, which is believed to have mutated into HIV in humans. Because Koprowski's vaccine was also administered in Poland, Croatia, and Switzerland, where no early HIV infections were recorded, it is probably more likely that the first human contraction of HIV occurred through contact with chimpanzee blood in areas where chimpanzees are hunted for food. More radical in their claims of vaccine contamination are the dozens of conspiracy Web sites that accuse Jonas Salk, who developed the first polio vaccine with dead polio virus in 1954, and Albert Sabin, who one year later developed the oral vaccine with weakened polio cells, of advancing a Jewish plot to infect the Christian world. So I got my gamma globulin shot.

In talking with Dr. Kleist, I also confirmed my suspicion that members of the hepatitis family of viruses (A through E) are not related to each other except in their effect on the human body, which is that they inflame the liver, which is what *hepatitis* (from Greek) means. Other hepatitises are more dangerous, can cause death, must be treated aggressively with medicines, are transmitted mostly through blood. Infants in the United States today are vaccinated against hepatitis B as a matter of course. The vaccine for hepatitis A was only approved for general use in 1995, which explains why I hadn't gotten it before I first came to Uruguay in 1993 and why I had to get gamma globulin shots every three months. Hepatitis C can work undetected for several years until the liver is scarred or fails entirely. There is no vaccine against it. Both B and C may stay with a person for life, resurging at inopportune times. D and E are mysterious, the one needing the B virus to exist and the other appearing quite like A but not exactly. Hepatitises affect in greater proportions the same demographic groups that are at high risk for AIDS. And when your immune system is already crippled by AIDS, hepatitis of any strain can damage your liver's normal functioning and be quickly fatal.

The kids were basically fine after a couple of days, though they were still contagious and supposed to be resting, and I found that hepatitis A and its treatment are common knowledge in Uruguay. There is no medicine to combat the disease, only bed rest and a special diet that avoids oils and fats and sugars. People asked me all the time how I dealt with the kids, how I kept them still. Usually I said "barely" or "it's hard," never quite hitting on the right humorous response to give them, and I wonder now why I felt I had to be humorous. So my children spent a month at home, out of school, partly in bed, driving Karina and me crazy, while gamma globulin and I warded off the disease entirely, which was good in a practical way — I could help Karina with the kids — but which compounded the guilt I already felt. I had saved myself.

The dog suffered through two days of pain, wheezing, and valiant attempts to remain standing and awake, but these always ended in thudding falls and nails scratching quickly against the tile floor of the kitchen where we kept her because it was raining. Each day, in spite of the various medicines the veterinarian gave her, she got a little worse, and I was amazed that a body could hang on for that long. The diagnosis was heart and kidney failure and fluid in the lungs so that her blood was not properly oxygenated, did not filter properly in the heart, whose swollenness meant that its valves did not close properly. Pressure on her torso, from lying down for instance, made breathing even more difficult, and she strained forward, eyes bulging, nose wide, seeking air. Each breath bared her ribs through taut skin and short yellow hair, made a sucking, liquid sound, then she would hack ineffectually, trying to loose something to make breathing easy again, involuntary, reflex. The causes and effects tangled: she could barely lie down because that made her lung capacity smaller and put pressure on her swollen organs, so she could hardly sleep, so she could not recover, could not rest from the pain and strain, would stand for as long as she could will it until her body simply gave out, another crash to the floor, then a struggle to stand again and again and again.

By Sunday afternoon we had lost hope. The dog could no longer stand. She couldn't even lie down correctly. She just splayed her legs wherever they fell and gasped for air. Animals don't get surgery or morphine or respirators in Uruguay, so we decided, on the veterinarian's advice, to put her to sleep, which he did by administering a relaxant and then the lethal injection right there on our front stoop while Karina held the dog's head, crying, gently whispering and caressing her fur, while I ran to get paper towels to wipe up the blood from the injection, while the veterinarian snapped off his latex gloves and stowed his medicines and poisons in a tackle box, while the dog strained, slowly convulsing, holding on, conscious but leaving, stretched full length pointing, wanting air, and inner mysterious processes circulating replenishing growing, for far too long, I thought, and then was still. There are people who see this sort of thing all the time, but I think I had never before witnessed the death of any living creature bigger than a breadbox. I had long ago given up crying over dead dogs, but I cried for Karina.

Then Karina is gone to the pet cemetery to witness the burial, to say goodbye one last time, and I am home with the kids, struggling to keep them still, not fighting, out of the fridge, with slippers on their feet. A glance out the front window toward the gate reminds me that the dog is gone. The trees are losing their leaves in May; the winds are bringing cold from the South. Pato's shoelace is still hanging tied in a square knot from the window latch in the kitchen, in case we have to give another i.v. It's raining steadily and gray and I can't get it out of my head how small the dog looked, bent, doubled over and bundled in a white sheet tied at the corners leaning against a tree.

Finity

Oh, what a brave faculty is hope, which,
in a mortal subject and in a moment, usurps
infinity, immensity, eternity!

MONTAIGNE "Of Names"

GRAPES, APPLES

There are 172 grapes in the bag I bought from my local Smith's supermarket. One-hundred-sixty of them look to be in good shape, four of them are undeveloped, six of them are deflated, and two were hiding underneath the drain in the sink where

I washed them yesterday, thus upsetting the nicely round number (a prime number multiplied by ten!) I thought I had.

So I returned to Smith's to buy another bag of grapes. On the fruit stand just inside the automatic doors, I found only eleven bags of grapes: seven green and four purple. They were on sale for a dollar a pound (called "10 for $10" by the store). I picked the bag that looked healthiest. I noticed nine escaped purple grapes and two escaped green ones on the purple cardboard padding below. To the side, on the next stand, there were ninety-nine small red delicious apples at seventy-nine cents a pound. Beside those there were more than ninety-nine (it was obvious; I chose not to count) golden delicious apples, and even more gala apples, each at seventy-nine cents a pound, too. Next on down the line were eighteen large mangoes (10 for $10; save 29¢!), then thirty-four large pink grapefruits (99¢ a pound; I picked up two). Around the back, on another stand, there were Jonagold apples, cameo apples, other batches of golden delicious and gala apples, red delicious apples, Braeburn apples, Granny Smith apples, pink lady apples, ambrosia apples. There were five- and ten-pound bags of apples for discounted prices. There were Seneca-brand apple chips. Not far away there were twelve brands of apple juice and cider in bottles (including organic, sparkling, and light varieties). Near those were four brands of applesauce, some in individual-sized plastic cups, some flavored with strawberry or cinnamon. In the freezer aisle there were three brands of frozen apple juice, not counting the unnatural pairings (mostly by Old Orchard, which had no solo apple juice) of apple with strawberry and kiwi, passion fruit and mango, cherry, raspberry, cranberry. There were apple pies and Apple Newtons and apple Pop-Tarts and apple Toaster Strudels.

Also, there were twenty-two more bags of grapes in the cooler on the sidewall of the produce section: eight green and fourteen purple. There was also the produce guy straightening up the piles of fruits and adding new ones and eyeing me a bit suspiciously as I stood counting grapes and grapefruits and apples, as I jotted down numbers and names on the back of my grocery list. So I left.

When I got home, I counted the grapes I had bought. There were 136, though they were much smaller and sourer than the other grapes. I didn't weigh them, but they seemed to occupy less than half the space the other grapes had occupied in the grape bowl.

These grapes, according to their bag, had traveled all the way from Chile, where it was now summer, to my Smith's super-market at the crossroads of Main Street and Redwood Road, on the border of Lehi and Saratoga Springs, Utah. Smith's is a Utah grocery store franchise, but it was recently subsumed by Kroger's, an Ohio chain. The Kroger conglomerate owns 2,515 grocery stores in thirty-seven states. All of them sell grapes and apples no matter the season.

PHYSICS, METAPHYSICS

When I was younger, I loved physics. My high school teacher, Mr. Altenderfer, made the world seem magical, yet knowable. His influence led me to finish a bachelor's degree in physics, though I had soured on it by the time I was done. Rarely, during my high school years, did we delve into metaphysics, the rea-sons why, the unknown realms beyond knowledge, the specula-tions and imaginations. But we thought, as do we all, about the universe and time. When we experimented, we learned that we approximated a closed system, a section of everywhere and everywhen that we could, in some measure, control, or at least fit in our minds. Or so we thought. But the boundaries were flimsy and tempting. First we wondered about influences from outside the system (the experiment), then outside that system (the whole lab or school), then outside that system (the planet), outside that system (the solar system), etc. (the galaxy, visible space, mathematical models of the universe back to the moment of the Big Bang). The thought experiment was dizzying.

> If the universe is everything, and scientists say that the universe is expanding, what is it expanding into?
>
> STEPHEN WRIGHT

Soon, college brought me advanced physics and late-night conversations with roommates, so I thought, too, of infinite knowledge and time, the paradox of free will, the irresistible force meeting the immovable object, a boulder so large that God cannot lift it, the mystery of prayer. It brought, as Edmund Burke says, a "sort of delightful horror, which is the most genuine effect and truest test of the sublime."

But I am not thinking, now, of the infinite, only the finite, or perhaps the subsection of the finite that is very large, in number or quantity, those things we must, of necessity, receive piecemeal, "detached and subdivided": all the grapes in the world, all the grains of sand on the beach, all the stars in the sky, all the people who ever lived.

ABRAHAM'S SEED

After Abram's nephew Lot moved to Sodom, and Abram to Mamre (the town of Bethel wasn't big enough for the two of them), God said to Abram:

> I will make thy seed as the dust of the earth: so that if a man can number the dust of the earth, then shall thy seed also be numbered.
>
> Genesis 13:16

Later, in a vision, a revision:

> Look now toward heaven, and tell the stars, if thou be able to number them: and he said unto him, So shall thy seed be.
>
> Genesis 15:5

If I'm Abram, I'm thinking, since my wife Sarai is infertile and my only heir nowadays is my steward, Eliezer of Damascus, that this may be a trick: *If* a man can number the dust of the earth? *If* I be able to number the stars? And if he can't? If I be-n't?

Yet, as Paul tells us, Abram "against hope believed in hope, that he might become the father of many nations." Along the way, though, Abram probably thought less and less about the promise, or revised his expectations. He organized a guerrilla force and attacked by night to rescue Lot from Amraphel, king of Shinar, Arioch, king of Ellasar, Chedorlaomer, king of Elam, and Tidal, king of nations, who had taken him and his goods captive; he lay with Hagar, Sarai's Egyptian handmaid, who bore him a son, Ishmael ("a wild man; his hand will be against every man, and every man's hand against him"); he sealed the deal with God, changing his name to Abraham and getting circumcised at age ninety-nine, along with Ishmael, age thirteen, and all the men of his house; he debated with God, trying to save Sodom from destruction, whittling down God's request from fifty all the way to ten righteous, instigating that great theological debate, the problem of evil, why does the Lord allow the humble to bear iniquity, why do bad things happen to good people? I like Abraham here in his impertinence:

> Shall not the Judge of all the earth do right?
>
> Genesis 18:25

He's got him there, so God reneges. Then in unwavering humility, Abraham begins the barter:

> Behold now, I have taken upon me to speak unto the Lord, which am but dust and ashes: Peradventure there shall lack five of the fifty righteous: wilt thou destroy all the city for lack of five?
>
> Genesis 18:27–28

Abraham doesn't back down, in spite of his tiptoeing. As it was, there were only four righteous there, and maybe not even that many. As chapter 19 opens, we cut scene to Lot's house in Sodom, where Lot is offering his virgin daughters to appease an angry mob that wants to "know" the two angels staying there; later, as Lot and his family fled, Lot's wife looked back and became a pillar of salt. A few days later, in a cave near Zoar, his two daughters (who were saved, despite their father's reckless endangerment) got him drunk and lay with him "that [they might] preserve seed of [their] father."

Back at Mamre, God had renewed the promise with Abraham, saying this time for sure that the line would continue through his wife, now called Sarah. And look: when Sarah heard it, she first responded not with desiccated joy in the continuation of the lineage. No,

> Sarah laughed within herself, saying, After I am waxed old shall I have pleasure, my lord being old also?
>
> Genesis 18:12

The number of stars in the heavens or motes of dust on the earth is, for all intents and purposes, uncountable, incomprehensible. "For all intents and purposes": now there's a phrase I bet most of us got wrong the first few times we heard it (like "supposably" or "all [of] the sudden" or "just assume" or those phrases that have given way to the masses' confusions: "chomping at the bit" for "champing at the bit" or "spitting image" for "spit and image"). For me, and for lots of people, it was "for all intensive purposes." While I am, nowadays, an incorrigible stickler on questions of grammar and usage, I hold a fondness and a potential for "for all intensive purposes," which seems not only more up-to-date but more, I don't know, *intense.* What power one would wield if one could marshal *all* intensive purposes. It sounds like the plot of a G.I. Joe episode.

In any case, knowing how many stars there are is a divine attribute, not a trait of mere mortals:

He telleth the number of the stars; he calleth them all by their names. Great is our Lord, and of great power: his understanding is infinite.

Psalms 147:4–5

So . . .

HOW MANY STARS ARE THERE IN THE UNIVERSE?

Tell a man that there are 400 billion stars and he'll believe you. Tell him a bench has wet paint and he has to touch it.

STEPHEN WRIGHT

Wright's funny, but he's not right. He has underestimated by roughly a factor of 10^{12} (so take his 400 billion and *multiply* it by another 400 billion and you're in the right neighborhood). Of course, no one knows exactly how many stars there are in the universe. Where I live, and likely where you live, too, there are only thousands of stars visible to the naked eye. With a basic telescope and some better darkness, you could see millions more. The European Space Agency, which in 2007 launched an infrared space observatory to count galaxies and measure their luminosity (to allow better approximations of — you guessed it — how many stars there are in the universe) estimates that there are between 10^{22} and 10^{24}. The notation does the number an injustice. There it is, so compact that it fits in a space on the page smaller than your pinkie fingernail. And yet it is a number beyond imagining.

There is no way that Abraham could have that many descendants. According to calculations by Carl Haub of the Population Reference Bureau (prb.org), assuming that the first humans set foot on earth about fifty thousand years ago, and "guesstimating" (his word) population sizes, birth rates, and life expectancies through the ages, there have been 106,456,367,669 people born on Earth in all of history. That's just over 10^{11}, with a few billion of those people living before Abraham (scholars estimate that he lived more or less around 2000 BC). So, even if somehow everybody on earth today were descended from Abraham, you'd still have to multiply everybody who's ever lived by everybody who's ever lived (I can't fit this into my mind, can you?) to get anywhere close to the number of stars in the universe.

And, mathematically, everybody on earth *could* be descended from Abraham. First of all, even though God's promise was extended through Isaac, Sarah's son, Abraham had a total of eight sons. Ishmael and Isaac were the first two, but after Sarah died, Abraham married Keturah, who bore him Zimran, Jokshan, Medan, Midian, Ishbak, and Shuah. Ishmael had twelve sons, and although Isaac only had two (Esau and Jacob, later called Israel), Israel had twelve sons. The Bible record is very scant on how many daughters each of these patriarchs had, though daughters are mentioned. So they got a good start on populating the whole world, and despite the older brothers' attempts to get rid of Joseph, all twelve of Abraham's great-grandsons through the promised line survived well into adulthood, so it's even mathematically possible that we might all be descended from Sarah.

Here's how it would work: we assume that Abraham lived four thousand years ago. It doesn't matter much how many people were alive then, but let's say it was 20 million. One generation after Abraham, there are at least eight people with Abraham's genes. One generation after that there are at least fourteen, and likely thirty-two or more. Next generation, it's something like sixty-four. Even if everybody slows down, a few great-grandchildren never marry, others marry their own relatives, a few get killed in battle, etc., Abraham's descendants are becoming a greater percentage of the population, even as the whole population grows. (This is not a takeover: their Abrahamic genes are becoming less prominent, too, mixed with the genes of others.) Estimating conservatively, within fifty generations, everyone on earth can be descended from Abraham.

If this sounds unlikely, it's because human beings are willful, passionate creatures, marrying for alliances and common beliefs; we're not loose molecules cast about by natural forces. Abraham's descendants may not have moved to every part of the world; they may have decided to marry their own (the Bible tells us as much); they may have been shunned and persecuted and systematically killed, thus keeping them from intermarrying with other groups of people.

If I may briefly attend to a common objection I've encountered, from bright people no less: in response to my claim that we may all be descendants of Abraham, they've "corrected" me with "You're assuming Abraham was the only one having children back then." Not at all. The fact is, we might all be descendants of *everybody* who lived four thousand years ago. Heck, if you traipse mathematically *backward* along your family tree, you'll find that you could have had 10^{60} forebears two hundred generations ago (Abraham's time). All indications tell us that that's fifty-two orders of magnitude more than the total number of people alive then, and it's forty-nine orders of magnitude more than Haub's estimate for all the people who have *ever* lived. We each have two parents and four grandparents and eight great-grandparents, and so on, but somewhere back there, people must start marrying relatives (close or distant) and causing significant overlap in their great-great-great-greats. Sometimes it happens close up: for instance, one pair of my wife's grandparents were cousins, which gives her only fourteen great-great-grandparents while I have sixteen. If there are no other close relatives who married, then Karina has twenty-eight great-great-great grandparents to my thirty-two, fifty-six four-greats to my sixty-four, and so on. And the neat mathematics of it all can get mighty complicated with second marriages or unmarried pregnancies or incests or any number of sexual variations.

Nevertheless, even if all of the people in the world today *were* somehow descended from Abraham, and even if we all have been for several generations, you're still ridiculously far from the number of stars in the universe. So maybe, one thinks, God was referring to the visible stars, which numbered, back in the day, with essentially no light pollution but without telescopes, as long as you took a few steps away from the fire, only in the tens-of-thousands range. Abraham probably achieved that within three hundred years, even if you stick to just Sarah's descendants.

Which might be all right, except for the problematic dust promise, and the next iteration of the metaphor, after Abraham's trial, Isaac's near-sacrifice:

> By myself have I sworn, saith the LORD, for because thou hast done this thing, and hast not withheld thy son, thine only son: That in blessing I will bless thee, and in multiplying I will multiply thy seed as the stars of the heaven, and as the sand which is upon the sea shore; And in thy seed shall all the nations of the earth be blessed.
>
> Genesis 22:16–17

"The sand which is upon the sea shore," eh? By the way, why is it impossible to starve in the desert? Because of all the *sand which is* there. (I am a martinet even for *that* and *which*, restrictive and nonrestrictive clauses, but when the King James translators choose *which* over *that*, it is not overcorrection or affectation; it is a setup for a joke.)

ARCHIMEDES' SAND RECKONER

Notice that God did not challenge anybody to *count* grains of sand, but Pindar, the Greek lyric poet laureate of the Olympics, did, at least indirectly:

> The sand escapes numbering
> — or —
> None can count the ocean's sand
> — or —
> Go, count each sand-grain on the storm-swept beach.
>> "Olympian Ode 2" (depending on your translation)

One gets the idea that this was a common expression of vastness, meant to cast the mind to awe, to humble the hearer. In fact, similar phrases alluding to the innumerability of sand appear in Aristophanes' play *The Archanians* and in the *Iliad*. But Archimedes, the Syracusan philosopher, mathematician, geometrician, etc., didn't buy it. He knew a good challenge when he saw one, and decided that you *could* number all the sand. This is the same man who supposedly ran naked through the streets shouting "Eureka!" after discovering that he displaced water equal to his body's volume. Thus, he could test whether King Hiero's new crown was made of pure gold or if it was adulterated with less-dense silver (as was the case, apparently). This story, apocryphal or not (it comes to us through Vitruvius's *De Architectura*, written in Rome circa 27 BC, at least two centuries after it would have happened), is yet one more example of the subconscious mind working overtime, grasping at everything within its reach and experience, finding answers or connections in unexpected places, when weighted by a ponderous ponderance.

Regarding sand, though, Archimedes set out not to count but to calculate. First, he established estimates for the size of the earth (he erred by a factor of ten too big) and, then — figuring, perhaps, *why not?* — for the size of the universe, which was not far off from the currently accepted size of our solar system. Next, because the numerical system currently at his disposal — which reached its upper limit at a *myriad*, or 10,000 — was insufficient for his calculations, he devised an exponential system (along the way discovering and proving that $10^a \times 10^b = 10^{a+b}$) that allowed him to notate ridiculously large numbers. Next, he calculated how many grains of sand were equivalent to a poppy seed, then how many poppy seeds fit into a 1-inch sphere, then how many fit into the universe. Given lots of room for errors of supposition (but not calculation), he determined that a sand-filled universe would contain approximately 10^{63} grains. He ended his explanation with this disclaimer:

> To the many who have not also had a share of
> mathematics I suppose that these will not appear readily

believable, but to those who have partaken of them and have thought deeply about the distances and sizes of the earth and sun and moon and the whole world this will be believable on the basis of demonstration.

Revising Archimedes' suppositions a bit, and approximating a lot of numbers, my father and I came up with a slightly more reasonable approximation for the number of grains of sand actually on the earth. Say that the earth is 25 percent land, and 1 percent of that land is sand to a depth of 10 feet. Each grain of sand is about 0.1 millimeters in diameter. Then you'd get about 1.5×10^{22} grains. If you don't believe that, John Lamb, a chemistry professor at Brigham Young University, had done his own calculations a few years back in preparation for a university devotional speech, and he sent me his scratch sheet. He may be more exact on his weights. Ten milliliters of sand, by his measurements, weigh 15.7715 grams, and thirty grains of sand weigh 0.00836 grams. This gives 56,590 grains in the 10 milliliters. Lamb assumes 10^6 kilometers of beach on earth at an average 10-meters width and 1-meter depth, which gives 5×10^{19} grains of sand on earth. That's almost five hundred times less than my father and I calculated, but either way, it's still too many descendants for Abraham.

This is all well and good, but to the mind, it really doesn't matter much if the exponent above and behind the 10 is 19 or 22 or 63 (though the latter is, in reality, *vastly* preponderant). The problem, it seems to me, is not so much a matter of the numbers on paper or the notation, but of conception, or of the logistics of real counting. My six-year-old daughter understands, fascinated, that counting is logical and additive, simply a matter of fitting a recursive linguistic pattern. But she gets tired soon after one hundred, and her mind wanders, and she decides she really doesn't want to count to two hundred or a million or fifty hundred thousand.

And realistically, much of the time when we're saying *infinite* what we really mean is "too big to count."

> There are scarce any things which can become the objects of our senses, that are really and in their own nature infinite.
>
> EDMUND BURKE *On the Sublime and Beautiful*

Still, the finite-but-extremely-vast is as fascinating, as dizzying, as discombobulating as any supposed infinite thing. Most of the time, I take a deep and perverse kind of pleasure from thinking on the superfinite, trying to fit it in my mind as I close my eyes and let my fingers find the keys they know are beneath them, crafting words to give voice to impossible ideas that we've tamed by reducing them to figures, other symbols, like words, meant to encapsulate some essence, some idea in easily portable, transferable packets of *meaning*. At other times, the mental exercise can be downright discouraging, the sheer innumerability of things becoming a weight on the soul, a snuffer leading to a sort of existential despair. What hope can there be under the barrage of uncontrollable things? What exit can we slip through when the numbers begin piling up, unaccountably, uncountably, demanding attention or comprehension? Indeed, the vertigo of numbered things can be such that one begins to wonder if any thing is truly infinite. Perhaps only ideas.

But if there *is* one infinite thing, you might think it's Apollo's herd of sun cattle. No one would blame you for such an assumption. But again, Archimedes would be there to prove you and the scholars of the Library of Alexandria wrong with one of the most complex computational arithmetic problems ever devised. It reads like a GRE analytical problem written by a mathematician on the verge of breakdown:

If thou art diligent and wise, O stranger, compute the number of cattle of the Sun, who once upon a time grazed on the fields of the Thrinacian isle of Sicily, divided into four herds of different colours, one milk white, another a glossy black, a third yellow, and the last dappled. In each herd were bulls, mighty in number according to these proportions: Understand, stranger, that the white bulls were equal to a half and a third of the black together with the whole of the yellow, while the black were equal to the fourth part of the dappled and a fifth, together with, once more, the whole of the yellow. Observe further that the remaining bulls, the dappled, were equal to a sixth part of the white and a seventh, together with all of the yellow. These were the proportions of the cows: The white were precisely equal to the third part and a fourth of the whole herd of the black; while the black were equal to the fourth part once more of the dappled and with it a fifth part, when all, including the bulls, went to pasture together. Now the dappled in four parts were equal in number to a fifth part and a sixth of the yellow herd. Finally the yellow were in number equal to a sixth part and a seventh of the white herd. If thou canst accurately tell, O stranger, the number of cattle of the Sun, giving separately the number of well-fed bulls and again the number of females according to each colour, thou wouldst not be called unskilled or ignorant of numbers, but not yet shalt thou be numbered among the wise.

But come, understand also all these conditions regarding the cattle of the Sun. When the white bulls mingled their number with the black, they stood firm, equal in depth and breadth, and the plains of Thrinacia, stretching far in all ways, were filled with their multitude.

Again, when the yellow and the dappled bulls were gathered into one herd they stood in such a manner that their number, beginning from one, grew slowly greater till it completed a triangular figure, there being no bulls of other colours in their midst nor none of them lacking. If thou art able, O stranger, to find out all these things and gather them together in your mind, giving all the relations, thou shalt depart crowned with glory and knowing that thou hast been adjudged perfect in this species of wisdom.

If you just skimmed over those last two quoted paragraphs, that's fine; you've demonstrated what I'm talking about: our inability to sort through so much information, our incapacity to parse such complex interrelations.

The solution to the first part of the problem is 50,389,082 (according to Drexel University mathematics professor emeritus Chris Rorres), but to be numbered among the wise, one must also solve the second part. From 1889 to 1893 the three members of the Hillsboro (Illinois) Mathematical Club, following the 1880 work of one A. Amthor, worked out the first 31 digits (though they were wrong on the last two) and the last 12 digits of the solution. In 1965 researchers at the University of Waterloo, in Canada, needed nearly eight hours of number-crunching computer time to determine all 206,545 digits of the solution, which can be expressed approximately as $7.760271 \times 10^{206544}$ and which can be calculated in barely a couple of seconds on today's home computers.

Still, Archimedes claims that for you to be adjudged perfect in this species of wisdom, you must "gather [all these things] together in your mind," and I don't think anyone can do that.

JAMES BURKE, NEURAL CONNECTIONS

OK, theoretically, it *may* be possible. In his recent talk at Brigham Young University, James Burke, author and host of the BBC program *Connections*, predictably decried the limitations that result from the inherent exclusions of academia, pointing out that, given each person's 100 billion neurons, there are more ways a message can go through the brain than there are atoms in the universe. There are more pathways to connection than there are physical things to connect.

Burke also argued against the compartmentalization of academic studies, the Cartesian reduction of the whole into manageable systems. Similarly, or asymptotically, Gary Saul Morson, in his treatment of Lao Tzu, expresses the impossibilities of a closed system:

> The very fact that we are in the world . . . makes it impossible to understand it. We are trapped at a moment of time so we cannot see the world from the perspective of eternity. We are entangled by language, by the very categories of thought.
>
> "The Aphorism: Fragments from the Breakdown of Reason"

Perhaps we are summoning (again) Archimedes, who claimed that he could move the earth if he but had a place to stand on. Or we are echoing Herman Dooyeweerd, the twentieth-century Dutch philosopher, who posited (if not originated) the metaphorical concept of an "Archimedean point" outside the system from which to understand the totality of philosophical or theological meaning. Yet the theory has no place in reality. It is a hazy, impossible concept, and perhaps not even a desirable one. This, it seems vibrantly clear to me, is why we essay, why I want to be a polymath examiner-of-the-world, a thinker (and doesn't everybody?). This is also why I laugh at our characterizations of the great thinkers who came before. We break Archimedes into his components as suits our needs: mathematician, physicist, engineer, astronomer, philosopher. That last label might fit best: a lover of wisdom and knowledge.

GENGHIS KHAN, NIALL NOIGÍALLACH, BRIGHAM YOUNG

Speaking of lovers, return with me, if you will, to our consideration of progeny. As the ninth of eleven children, Brigham Young, whose name my university bears, was no stranger to large families. Contemporary reports assure us that he was reluctant to practice polygamy when the doctrine was announced by Joseph Smith, but you could say he made the most of it when he finally decided to go along (his first wife, Miriam Work, had died in 1833, before Young married his second wife, Mary Angell, the following year, and then, beginning in 1842, many other women).

It is a bit difficult to figure out how many children Brigham Young had. Even Latter-day Saint church historians seem not to know, though all the ones I talked to figure it's a very big number. Several Web sites and at least one official church book give the number of children as fifty-seven, by sixteen of his wives (another difficult statistic to gather; it is likely that he married as many as sixty-one women). The Brigham Young Family Association was unresponsive to my queries. But let's say that Brigham Young has thousands, nearing tens of thousands, of descendants nowadays. The association Web site lists, in addition to Young, over 2,000 surnames of his descendants, many of them shared by several people. Plus, there are 808 Youngs, and they don't even list Brother Brigham's most athletic left-handed heir, NFL Hall-of-Famer Steve Young.

If you've been curious about such things, as I have been lately, you might have heard about the numerous modern-day progeny of Niall Noigíallach, a.k.a. Niall of the Nine Hostages, a fifth-century Irish king, sometimes dismissed as simply legendary, sometimes credited with kidnapping the British teenager with the charming name who would return a score of years later to drive out the snakes and convert the pagan Irish to Christianity through his clever trefoiled metaphor. In 2006 Daniel Bradley and a team of geneticists at Trinity College discovered a "distinctive genetic signature" on the Y chromosomes (which are passed from father to son) of 20 percent of men in northwestern Ireland (and 2 percent of men in New York City). This, Bradley concludes, points to some common ancestor, who might just as well be Niall (the chromosome abnormality is common among those whose families claim descendancy from him), who gained his nickname when he consolidated his realm by taking nine hostages from local royal families.

In any case, *some* ancient Irish man with the wherewithal to spread the fruits of his loins far and wide has approximately 3 million male descendants today, putting him second (so far) to Genghis Khan, who, despite his much later start (the thirteenth century), is believed to be the progenitor of approximately

16 million men today, roughly one-half of one percent of the world's current population. Granted, this is all conjecture, since neither Niall nor Genghis is available to give a DNA sample. But given the Khans' prolific procreative practices, and the strange coincidence that an isolated group of Genghis-descended Pakistanis displays the same genetic mutation found in 8 percent of the Mongolian population, scientists (and I) believe it very likely that Genghis Khan is the man. No word on whether his cheery disposition has also survived intact.

CHILDREN, POPULATION

> I believe the children are our future.
> WHITNEY HOUSTON "Greatest Love of All"

Karina and I have four children. This, in the grand scope of things, is not entirely strange or out of sorts. Both Karina and I come from four-children families. My father, too. Her father's family included eight children. (Our mothers are both only children but didn't like growing up without siblings.) One problem, though, in a cold-hearted zero-sum view of resource management, is that we are healthy and relatively wealthy, thus our four children are still alive and can be expected to live well into adulthood. They, like we, consume more than their fair share of the earth's bounty, even, apparently, when we lived in a small house in Uruguay recently, didn't own a car, rode bicycles and walked (or rode buses to travel long distances), bought almost entirely local produce, rarely ate processed, preservative-laden foods (they were too expensive), recycled much of our trash, etc. According to myfootprint.org, we'd still need 2.2 planets for everyone to live like my family did in Uruguay. And the fact is, we're no longer living there, we're living in Utah, where water is dammed and apportioned, where victuals are imported, and where so many people drive cars up and down the valley that in winter, exhaust is trapped between mountains in an unhealthy "inversion."

Many of my friends who received the news of our fourth child's birth recently have responded with some version of "whoa!" in both of its senses. Mark Halliday, who feels strongly about such things, once wrote a poem called "Population," which goes, in part:

> we can make babies galore, baby:
> let's get on with it. Climb aboard.
> Let's be affirmative here, let's be pro-life for God's sake
> how can life be wrong?
> . . .
> If you have ten kids they'll be so sweet —
> ten really sweet kids! Have twelve!
> What if there were 48 pro baseball teams,
> you could see a damn lot more games!

He's made his point on the page, so he doesn't really need to confront people about it, but he does, though in slightly more tactful terms. When Karina and I were expecting our third child, he said, "You know, now they're going to outnumber you." Mark has two kids, though with two different wives, which can be better or worse, depending on your views. In his view, that's two new people out of three existing ones, which is a step in the right direction. In fact, he says, he's "taken one other guy out of commission": his son's stepfather, who has no children of his own, so even better. When we'd had number four, he expressed his condolences, then, during our farewell niceties (he had come to visit BYU) slipped in "Now, if you e-mail to tell me about child number five, I'm going to have you committed," or some such revealing threat veiled in humor. I told him not to worry, though, of course, he's already been worrying.

According to the CIA, which keeps an online Factbook on every country in the world, as well as a page on "The World," there were 6,679,272,131 people as of July 2008. Every year, global population is growing by 1.167 percent. Not so long ago, in 1820, Earth had only about 1 billion human inhabitants. By 1930, when my grandfather was a young man, that number had doubled. By 1960, when my father was a high school junior, it was 3 billion. By my junior year, 1988, we'd reached 5 billion. We passed the 6 billion mark in 2000, when my son was two. By the time he's a junior in college, we're looking at 7.2 billion.

> Students of natural law hold that the birth, nourishment, and growth of each thing is the alteration and corruption of another.
>
> MONTAIGNE "One Man's Profit Is Another Man's Harm"

Eduardo Galeano, who writes exuberantly against United States imperialism and resource-hogging, but whom I don't know quite as well as Halliday, and who therefore buries his spoken opinions deeper, expressed his surprise when I told him we had four children (we'd had only two the last time we met), then turned philosophical: "Your wife must be a very strong woman. There are certain things only a mother can do, no matter how theoretically feminist a man pretends to be." His daughter, a lawyer, has three children of her own. He doesn't know how she manages.

Even complete strangers, in Uruguay at least, offer their guidance, in the metaphorical language of a dead-end economy (which may drive the message home more soundly). The guy my father-in-law hired to drive us home from the airport across town: "It's time to close the factory." The taxi driver who took us from Montevideo to the beach-town Atlantida: "The factory's supply is outstripping demand." The two guys at the

street bazaar who sold me a decorative hanging lamp made out of an old wagon wheel: "That factory's time has come." I'm varying their sayings here, for literary purposes — call it creative license in translation — but really, they had the same exact line rehearsed: "It's time to close the factory."

> Dealing in multiplication
> And we still can't feed everyone.
>
> EDDY GRANT "Electric Avenue"

It is small talk now, unintended and unimportant, the kind of harmless banter that means nothing, yet it is strange to me, this advising, which constitutes a meddling in the most private and most sacred part of a person's life: not only sex but procreation. My friend John Bennion tells how he once met an acquaintance in the hallway at the University of Houston who, asking about John's wife's fifth pregnancy, said, "You do know why this happens, don't you?" John tells the story deadpan, without a clue to the motives or the seriousness of the inquisitor.

FORBIDDEN FRUIT

The Bible never specifies what fruit it was that Adam and Eve, tempted by the serpent, partook of. Some Jewish scholars believe it was a pomegranate or grapes; Muslim tradition holds that it was a banana. But for Christians, thanks to artists' renderings, perhaps first in Hugo van der Goes's 1470 *The Fall of Man*, today "forbidden fruit," where I live, and likely where you live, too, is almost always synonymous with "apple."

It is also almost always synonymous with "sex," because, hey, eating an apple isn't a sin. There is also that bit about being fruitful and multiplying, plus they were naked, so it makes

sense to equate this Original Sin with sex. Currently, the opening sequence of the television show *Desperate Housewives* takes
advantage of this common association: we see a Monty Python-
esque adaptation of one of Lucas Cranach the Elder's sixteenth-
century *Adam and Eve* paintings; Eve receives a bright red apple
from the mouth of the snake coiled in the tree branches above;
Adam receives a crushing blow from a hippo-sized apple that
falls from beyond the frame; apples fall in a steady precipita-
tion: apples everywhere symbolizing sensuality, freedom from
fidelity, licentious liberation, recalling Eve's evolution, Adam's
atomization, the serpent's sequestration for setting us free.

Then they knew they were naked, were driven out of para-
dise, sent to toil in the harsh world. In this, the story of our
collective first memory, Adam and Eve ate the apple and were
thereby banished, separated from their Father.

PLUMS, FLUX

It is tempting to revisit metaphors when their symbols are
literally before us — beyond fructiferous multiplications: fruits
of labors, by their fruits ye shall know them, when saw we
thee an hungered, and fed thee? One sultry day in Uruguay,
my neighbor Lemes asked my mission companion Solomon
and me for help picking plums from two trees in his yard.
They were delicious, so sweet and so . . . not yet cold . . . and
brightly colored, and they came off their twigs easily with a
gentle tug. We sat on branches eating plums in the trees, we
let the overripe plums fall to the dogs, we gathered buckets
full of plums. When we were done, Lemes sent us with our
payment, a white plastic bag of plums. We wanted to save
them and eat them later, but we took them to José and Teresa's
shack, left them just inside the unlocked door, then slipped
quietly away.

This is just to say that part of the problem in counting things

like fruit is flux. There are plums growing on trees, being eaten, falling to the ground and rotting, losing their plumness. Dust we are, to dust we are returning. Second is a problem of definition: what constitutes a plum? an apple? a grape? Are the deflated, sour grapes viable? If I leave them outside to rot, when do they stop being grapes and become dirt? Another part of the problem, I think, is the result of communication. Ages ago, there were enough apples to feed the clan, enough grapes to eat and to make wine with; a few went bad and were thrown away; a few apples fell to the wasps and the dogs. Life was parochial and compartmentalized. There were cows and sows and rows of corn in plentiful supply. Their numbers were big but comprehensible. Once we see the expanse of this vast world, once we can know, almost instantly, the tragedies our brothers and sisters are facing halfway around the globe, once our fruits come to us no matter the season and from far away, more temperate places that grow things we could not have otherwise, we no longer wonder, at least not so much, how many there are of things. There is always enough of everything we could possibly want; it is automatically replenished on the shelves and bins, under the timely spray showers.

AVOGADRO

Not many people get numbers named after them. I can think of only one offhand: Avogadro, whose name derives from the Latin for "lawyer" or "advocate," which aptly describes what he was trained to do but not what he ended up doing.

We remember Avogadro today mostly because of his molecular hypothesis, which states that equal volumes of gas contain equal numbers of particles. Avogadro's Law combined with Charles's and Boyle's gives us the Ideal Gas Law, represented notationally as PV=nRT (Pressure times Volume equals n moles times the Universal Gas Constant [R, or 8.3145 J/mol K] times Temperature). Thus we can determine that a volume of 22.4 liters of any gas at 0°C and atmospheric pressure contains about 6.0221367×10^{23} particles (one "mole"). What does such a figure mean? Bob Everson, of Purdue University, offers this supposal:

> Let us suppose that the entire state of Texas, with an area of 262,000 square miles, were covered with a layer of fine sand 50 feet thick, each grain of sand being $1/100$ of an inch in diameter. There would then be Avogadro's number of sand particles in this immense sandpile.

At the same time, the quantity can seem quite manageable. Go drink yourself a pint of water. There went 25 moles of H_2O.

Avogadro's published works bore titles representative of their times; nevertheless, I feel a tug when I read them. For one thing, they're ridiculously long. For another, they're all *essays* or *memoirs*. His earliest postulation of the molecular hypothesis appeared in 1811's "Essai d'une manière de déterminer les masses relatives des molécules élémentaires des corps . . ." In 1814 he followed up with "Mémoire sur les masses relatives des molécules des corps simples . . ." His magnum opus was called *Fisica dei Corpi Ponderabili . . . (Physics of Ponderable Bodies)*. In 1820, after several years teaching at both the high school and university levels, Avogadro was appointed chair at the University of Turin of *fisica sublime*, which you almost don't want to translate. What would you translate it to? Sublime physics? *Fisica sublime* has the necessary rhythm, the dreamy tone of the unending, ever-approximated, never-known.

At the time Avogadro was doing his thinking (almost never experimenting), chemistry was far more mysterious than it is now. His generalization about the relationship between volume and particle quantity would prove essential for chemists to determine relative elemental weights. Still, Avogadro's work remained obscure during his lifetime, partly because he never traveled to Paris (Piedmont, his province, was under French governance during part of his lifetime), preferring instead to remain with his wife and six children in Turin. In 1860, four years after Avogadro died, Stanislao Cannizzaro presented his first arguments recognizing Avogadro's hypothesis as valid, but the idea still took over twenty years to really catch on. In 1869 Alexander Naumann christened the hypothesis "Avogadro's Law"; around the turn of the century, Jean Baptiste Perrin calculated Avogadro's number and named it in his honor.

According to Mario Morelli, a recent biographer, Avogadro's work consisted of

> speculations . . . based on others' experimental data, . . . ad hoc assumptions, and often daring conclusions.

Today he has been reduced to his law and the number that bears his name (he is commemorated every Mole Day, October 23 from 6:02 a.m. to 6:02 p.m. [get it? 6:02 10/23?]); still, this is a far greater legacy than the vast majority of his contemporaries. Amedeo Avogadro is considered a lawyer, statesman, statistician, meteorologist, chemist, physicist, mathematician, and philosopher: in other words, and by his own admission, an essayist.

MOZART, FALCO, HOT POTATOES, SOCKS

I suspect that Amedeo is the same name as Amadeus, whose most famous bearer, Mozart, inspired not only Eddie Van Halen and Valerie Bertinelli's son's name (Wolfgang) but the famous Falco song "Rock Me, Amadeus," which we listened to (whether we wanted to or not) for an entire year and which we still hear every now and then on '80s radio shows. I was living in Louisiana at the time, a transplant from New Jersey, learning little by little to say "sir" and "ma'am," but not "y'all," which I say now as often as I please, but which I said then only once, deep in the woods, at a Boy Scout camp, playing a game called Indian Village, because I wanted to disguise my voice and trick the other team. I associate the general vibe of that time in Louisiana with Falco's hit song, but more so, I associate it with one particular high school track meet, about an hour from Baton Rouge, when one of our team's two vans broke down and we had to remove all the equipment (poles, shots, discs, etc.) from the working van and pile everybody in, some kids on the floor, some sitting on laps or lying across the backs of a few rows of seats. All the ride home, it seems now, we sang "Rock Me, Amadeus," but with our own lyrics: "Hot potatoes, hot potatoes . . . hot potatoes / Hot potatoes, hot potatoes . . . hot potatoes," et cetera, ad nauseam, accompanied by up-and-down hand movements like we were tossing potatoes back and forth. Everybody was in on it, even the cool kids, who in other circumstances would not have let on that they liked the song, could not have legally participated in such immature tomfoolery. "Oh oh oh, hot potatoes!"

For the most part, these were good guys, even though they taunted me for wearing my socks pulled up to my knees. Also, the socks were gray and had colored stripes. This was too much for them, and they pulled at them to push my buttons. Where other groups of rebels might have yanked a kid's underwear to give him a wedgie, these guys were content to sidle up to me and pull down my socks. Nowadays my wife does the same thing, though my socks are no longer gray, they don't have colored stripes, and they only come up to my calves. Still, this is too high for her. She buys me those socks that don't even cover my ankles and expects me to wear them with shorts, like one of those fitness dancer fellows on daytime cable exercise shows. She says I look like an old man with my socks pulled up. I tell her at least they're not black socks, and at least I'm not wearing sandals.

> Everybody pulled their socks up.
> Everybody put their foot down.
>
> JOHN LENNON "I've Got a Feeling"

Michael Cooper, a multipurpose player (and defensive magician) on the Los Angeles Lakers basketball team, during this same time when I was in Louisiana, used to wear *his* socks pulled all the way up to his knees, and, at least as far as I knew, nobody gave *him* any guff. He began wearing his socks pulled high in 1973 at a league championship game where his Pasadena High School team played against El Rancho. This must have been big stuff, because the game was televised on NBC. He had a good reason for pulling those socks up. "My grandmother had cataracts," said Cooper . . .

> That game was the first time she was going to watch me play basketball, so she said, "Michael, you're going to have to do something to distinguish yourself from the others." So I pulled my socks up real high, so she could see me.

I've never thought beyond the name Amedeo before, which is to say I've taken it at face value, but recently, as I've noted the similarities between Amedeo and Amadeus, I've come to a sort of connection or revelation: that *Amadeus* must mean "Loves God." If it doesn't, it should. Let me check. OK, I'm back. Apparently, my suspicions were essentially correct: "Love of God." I learned, too, that Mozart was baptized Wolfgang Theophilus Mozart but preferred the Latin translation of his Greek middle name. The name *Wolfgang*, I suspect, means just what it sounds like: a gang of wolves. This, as Dave Barry would surely note, would make a great name for a band (a lot better than Steppenwolf, where there's only one wolf, and he's just steppin').

The name *Theophilus* ought to send any Christian straight to his Bible, where one Theophilus (probably a representative name used by Luke to address all believers, I was told once or twice in my catechism classes) is the addressee of both of Luke's books, the Gospel According to and the Acts of the Apostles. So I went right to my Bible. Often when I do something like this, I find, to my astonishment, a connection to my project, some symbol or metaphor, some uncanny correlation to the overall theme. But not in this case. In fact, Luke is resolutely anti-essayistic in his bearings. His purpose in writing, he says, is

> It seemed good to me also, having had perfect understanding of all things from the very first, to write unto thee in order, most excellent Theophilus, that thou mightest know the certainty of those things, wherein thou hast been instructed.
>
> Luke 1:3–4

Perfect understanding and certainty are also, like star telling, divine attributes, so far from realistic human experience as to seem dizzyingly undesirable. I enjoy my essaying too much for such absolutes. And besides, let's get real . . .

> Left and rites of passage
> Black and whites of youth
> Who can face the knowledge
> That the truth is not the truth?
> Obsolete absolute, yeah!
>
> NEIL PEART "Distant Early Warning"

How many centuries make up this moment I'm now living? How many airs form the air I breathe?

EDUARDO GALEANO *Days and Nights of Love and War*

While we may generally assume that Abraham's descendants
remained local for long stretches of time, were shunned at
other times, and were killed genocidally at yet another time, we
might conversely assume that the air, or at least the nitrogen,
expelled by Julius Caesar in his dying exclamation ("*Et tu,
Brute?*" or whatever it might have been) has been adequately
preserved and dispersed by wind and weather to an even distri-
bution of molecules throughout the atmosphere. At least that's
what John Allen Paulos argues in his book *Innumeracy*:

> Take a deep breath. Assume Shakespeare's account is
> accurate and Julius Caesar gasped "You too, Brutus"
> before breathing his last. What are the chances you just
> inhaled a molecule which Caesar exhaled in his dying
> breath? The surprising answer is that, with probability
> better than 99 percent, you did just inhale such a
> molecule.
>
> For those who don't believe me: I'm assuming
> that after more than two thousand years the exhaled
> molecules are uniformly spread about the world and
> the vast majority are still free in the atmosphere. Given
> these reasonably valid assumptions, the problem of
> determining the relevant probability is straightforward.
> If there are N molecules of air in the world and
> Caesar exhaled A of them, then the probability that
> any given molecule you inhale is from Caesar is A/N.
> The probability that any given molecule you inhale is
> not from Caesar is thus 1-A/N. By the multiplication
> principle, if you inhale three molecules, the probability

that none of these three is from Caesar is $[1\text{-}A/N]^3$. Similarly, if you inhale B molecules, the probability that none of them is from Caesar is approximately $[1\text{-}A/N]B$. Hence, the probability of the complementary event, of your inhaling at least one of his exhaled molecules, is $1\text{-}[1\text{-}A/N]B$. A, B (each about 1/30th of a liter, or 2.2×10^{22}), and N (about 10^{44} molecules) are such that this probability is more than .99. It's intriguing that we're all, at least in this minimal sense, eventually part of one another.

Even though Paulos misstates average breath volume (adult human lungs can contain between four and five liters, and an average breath is about ½ a liter, not 1/30, especially if you "take a deep breath," as Paulos directs), and 1/30 of a liter does not contain 2.2×10^{22} molecules (that's the number of molecules in *one* liter), his conclusion is not far off. Still ignoring the loss of free molecules to combinations (most notably O_2 to H_2O), Peter L. Renz, in a rebuttal and reworking of Paulos's calculation, derives an 84 percent probability that your most recent inhalation brought with it a molecule exhaled by Caesar. And even though Paulos doesn't give credit, the question may be traced to James Jean's 1942 *An Introduction to the Kinetic Theory of Gases*, and may be considered yet one more example of a Fermi problem, named after Enrico Fermi, whose theoretical and experimental work in atomic physics paved the way for the atom bomb; whose children, through their mother, were descendants of Abraham (which led to the family's emigration from fascist Italy); and who was well-known for his habit of making accurate order-of-magnitude calculations based on rough assumptions with little real data. In other words, he could envision a closed system for the sake of argument, ignoring outside effects and influences, and even though his calculations would be rife with errors, these would cancel out, and he would come up with approximations very close to more carefully calculated (or experimentally measured) answers. For instance, during the first atomic bomb test, on July 16, 1945, he dropped bits of paper on the ground and measured how far they were blown by the blast wind. From this, he estimated that the blast had the power of 10 kilotons of TNT, and he was not far off. Fermi's best-known problem is "How many piano tuners are there in Chicago?" which he posited to his students at the University of Chicago. Hans Christian von Baeyer solves the problem this way in *The Fermi Solution*:

> If the population of metropolitan Chicago is 3 million, an average family consists of four people and one third of all families own pianos, there are two hundred and fifty thousand pianos in the city. If every piano is tuned once every five years, fifty thousand pianos must be tuned each year. If a tuner can service four pianos a day, two hundred and fifty days a year, for a total of one thousand tunings a year, there must be about fifty piano tuners in the city.

The answer cannot be exact, but, given a glance at the Chicago yellow pages, von Baeyer says, it's in the ballpark. So I want to say that Fermi, and his disciples, despite their sometime need for hard calculations and precise answers, are essayists at heart, grappling with the vast, searching not for exactness but for approximate knowledge, hints and intimations.

Of course, there's nothing special about Caesar's last breath as compared to the last breaths of everyone else, or their first breaths, or their twelfth breath after they got out of bed on the morning of their eighteenth birthday. The point is that we're all breathing recycled air. For what it's worth, though, the likelihood of you breathing molecules from Thomas Edison's last breath is somewhat smaller, since, first of all, he died only in 1931, and, second of all, his son Charles captured much of it in a test tube that now resides in the Henry Ford Museum in Dearborn, Michigan. Ford apparently believed that a dying breath contained a person's departing soul. He convinced Charles to save the expiration, perhaps hoping to cheat death and reconstitute the essence of his friend at some later date.

REUNION

> To see a world in a grain of sand,
> And a heaven in a wild flower,
> Hold infinity in the palm of your hand,
> And eternity in an hour.
>
> WILLIAM BLAKE "Auguries of Innocence"

In all my years, I have been to only one family reunion. There have been other visits with my father's siblings and their families, and sometimes with his uncle Jim or his cousin Diane or her mother, Aunt Marge, but these were casual and partial. My mother had almost no relatives (one cousin, whom we called Aunt Terry, and that was it), and my father's family lived, for the most part (most of them, most of the time) in Wisconsin, while we lived, for the most part, in New Jersey. That one reunion happened in the mid-1980s in Milwaukee. Gathered together were the descendants of John and Emma Vander Heyden, my father's mother's parents. There were nearly a hundred people there. To me, they were nearly all strangers.

If we were to gather the descendants of my grandfather Patrick Charles Madden I for a convenient starting point, we would find his blood in twenty-four bodies, aged from a few months (my cousin's son) to sixty-four years (my father). There would be eight spouses adopted in, contributing their own families' genes to the mix in five cases. Two of the newest, a brother and sister who married two of my cousins, sister and brother, would have yet to participate in the offspring project. Nineteen of us would carry my grandfather's last name. Four of us would carry his first name; three of us would carry all of his names, followed by various Roman numerals, mostly *I*s.

> How many people are there in every family with the same name and surname?
>
> MONTAIGNE "Of Names"

The youngest seven among us, his great-grandchildren, would have received one eighth of their genes from him, enough for relatives on this side of the family to attribute their blue eyes or small ears or twinkling smile to him. Others, perhaps, would have received less visible traits: eyebrow configurations, narrow shoulders, or the right-ear-lower-than-the-left-ear thing. The jury is still out on whether we might be genetically predisposed to aspects of his personality or his talents, but it would seem so. He was a wry man, a bit befuddled by the world, an observant painter-in-watercolors.

As it is, Patrick Charles Madden I, who received his Roman numeral only when his wife refused to call their son Junior, died more than twenty years ago, before nine of us were born and before six of the spouses got a chance to meet their father- or grandfather-in-law. Seven more of us never *really* got to know him; Alzheimer's disease wore away his memory bit by bit until he no longer recognized his own children, then plum forgot how to speak, then fell down and broke a hip and disintegrated. I, his oldest grandchild, was lucky in that when I was little, we would visit him, and he lived with us for a brief time near the beginning of his Alzheimer's woes. He sang to me, drew me pictures of jack-o-lanterns and scarecrows, told me his stories and listened to my stories. But in the end, many of us didn't even make it to his funeral. I think I did not want to face death, or I was busy and interested in school and sports. He had been leaving us slowly for nearly a decade; essentially, he was already gone. From my family, my father and younger brother David made the trip by themselves.

So let's call it thirty-two people at the reunion. We tell stories about Grandpa, about how he was fascinated by the accuracy and rapidity of the brand-new thirty-cent tollbooths on the Tri-State Tollway, once musing that "If you put in only twenty-nine cents, that thing won't budge. And right away, too!" or about how he laughed with his boys when Tom discovered an apple on the "pear" tree he had bought years before (and about which he had liked to joke: "Karras still throws more shade than those trees he sold me"). Thirty-two people with some interest in this man who doesn't exist on the Internet or in anybody's books, who is as unknown by his great-grandchildren as his father is by me, who faded to a shell before he died. Thirty-two people: but even that small number is hard to determine, hard to keep in the mind. I certainly didn't know it before I began to write this, and I had to plot it out on paper; I couldn't simply enumerate in my head. On the margins, possible additions, there is Bill, no longer married to Aunt Lynne, father of Ryan and Sarah. There is Michelle, never married to Uncle Jeff, mother of Paul. I have a recent e-mail from Heather, Paul's wife, with pictures of their two children, Noah and Sophia; otherwise, I would not know how to count that branch of the family. I don't keep in touch at all with Ryan and Sarah, nor their mother, nor their younger sister Gabrielle, who must be about fourteen by now; the last time I saw her she was an infant. I had to hear it through the grapevine (my sister, who does a slightly better job maintaining contact, who's visited Aunt Lynne fairly recently) that Ryan and Sarah aren't yet married and have no children. We are scattered, outside each other's systems, strangers for years at a time.

And why this intense focus on the paternal-paternal line? Am I not also my mother and grandmothers and my mother's father and grandfathers? Yes, but indulge me, dear reader. We cleave unto them that are like us. Men find inspiration in men, boys look up to fathers, want to play catch and converse in the twilight, hear the similarities in their voices and radiate pride when they surpass them in height or in arm wrestling. And more so for me, who shares my father's and grandfather's name, and who gave the name to my son, too. And what a name it is, in any case: Patrick, of the Irish saint who was not Irish, from the Latin for *patriarch*. So is it any wonder that I follow my urge to essay to understand my father's father, the father of my name; or Abraham, the father of many nations, the first of the great biblical patriarchs?

FIN

> But praise falls in with surfeit . . .
> For sands cannot be counted,
> And how many joys
> This man has brought his fellows, who can say?
>
> PINDAR "Olympian Ode 2"

As for me, all this essaying about vast quantities and procreation has got me dreading the conversation I must have, three years hence, I suppose, with my son, to explain to him the mechanisms of human reproduction, to instruct him in what he must do to create that Patrick Charles Madden V he sometimes says he wants (the apples have not fallen far from their respective trees). I am not so squeamish about the details as about the admission. I remember the conversation my father had with me, in the car on the way home from a Boy Scout camping trip: there is a winding road cutting through grassy hills, a frozen scene, perhaps the view at the moment I realized what he was going to say. I knew it all already, had gathered it in bits and pieces ever since some kid I knew told me his mother told him. We were in an alcove of branches under the bushes in my back yard, in the *Land of the Lost* cave, as I called it. I couldn't believe what he said, but I couldn't disprove it, either. I was seven or eight.

Thus, I also wonder at my origins, at the cosmic coincidence that my father's gravest mistake, down the line, gave birth to me. He had quit college, midway through his senior year, because he wanted to change his major from chemical engineering to music. He left school, failed (to show up for) his exams, went to work for a friend of an uncle pouring concrete basements in Milwaukee, and was almost immediately drafted to fight in Vietnam. Along the way, he was trained in electronics repair at Fort Monmouth, New Jersey. On weekends, he went into New York City, to Cardinal Spellman's Servicemen's Club, where he played ping-pong against my mother, a spry girl from Brooklyn, the only girl who could beat him.

There, too, in my wonderings is my grandfather, Patrick I, in training at Camp Polk, Louisiana, soon to leave for the European theater; his bride arrives from Milwaukee by bus, they are married on May 9, 1942, though they can't then remain together long. If you call it biological imperative or animal instinct or machismo — that night in the army housing or a nearby hotel when my father was conceived — I will sock you in the jaw. That scientific determinism is to me only a secular Calvinism, robbing my forebears of their free will, tracing back the results to their inevitabilities. There is something more here, more than a man desperate and mechanically driven to pass on his genes, to ensure the continuance of his line, something Darwin never theorized, though he may have known it with his own wife, or imagining his own grandparents. There is love, yes, and there are passionate rumblings and urgings. There is an abyss of the unknowable, the impossibility of a future, 405,099 American soldiers just like him who wouldn't return, millions more around the world returned to the earth with a bullet in the chest, a foot blown to bits, a torn-off limb. I imagine they were scared and in love, my grandparents, frantic for every moment they could steal from uncertainty. If my grandmother was the apple of my grandfather's eye, and my father was then only a twinkle in his father's eye, then I, III, was that imperceptible twinkle within the reflected light diffused from the deep red skin of the apple after he's shined it on his sleeve, as he brings it to his mouth to take a bite. I was a distant, vague notion, never voiced, but perhaps thought of, within that word *grandson*, or within that roomy name *Patrick Charles Madden*.

Our causes can't see their effects.

NEIL PEART "Natural Science"

Then he was gone to Europe until my father was two.

I had not thought of this until now: my father was named by his mother while her husband was far away fighting. I never met her, but I think I have caught a window into her soul: that she named him Patrick Charles Madden II just in case, or to ensure something, to stave off the telegram, to keep her husband, her hope against hope, alive no matter what. While in Europe he was shot at and captured by German forces in France, yet he returned in one piece while hundreds of thousands just like him returned in pine boxes or not at all. Why them and not him?

Besides Abraham's plea for Sodom, the other great — the greatest — biblical grapple with the problem of evil is the story of Job, who lost everything but his faith. His philosophical arguments with his friends, his justifications of his worthiness and righteousness, revealed a different Holy Father, one more like me: sick of the complaining, sick of explaining, raging against incomprehension and vain words:

> Where wast thou when I laid the foundations of the earth? declare, if thou hast understanding.
>
> Job 38:4

In the end, God never puts to rest the problem of evil; his response, while convincing in its ethos, amounts to "because I said so." So we're left back where we started, but perhaps we're left with a friend and example in Job, who, in spite of his superhuman longsuffering, seems utterly human in his questioning. Elie Wiesel, in his Nobel Prize acceptance speech, praises Job's fidelity *and* his chutzpah:

> Job was determined not to repudiate the creation, however imperfect, that God had entrusted to him. . . . The source of his hope was memory.

When we plumb the depths of memory, when we redis-cover those earliest imprints and connections, we often find that our first recollections are traumas: unexpected pain, grief, shocks, or surprises. My own first memory is me on a gurney trying to fool the doctor who explained that the mask he was placing over my face would make me sleep. I closed my eyes and breathed shallowly, not wanting to really lose conscious-ness, wanting to trick him and thereby avoid the operation (for a hernia, I learned later). My sister, Kathleen, remembers hearing but not comprehending the blaring of our home fire alarm; she was in the bathroom, standing on a step stool, with soap on her hands, when Dad burst in, grabbed her, ran her downstairs, and dropped her on the driveway next to me. My brother David remembers falling down the stairs and "cracking

[his] head open" (as our mother, and probably your mother, too, used to say). Dan, my youngest brother, also cracked his head open (on the corner of an end table in a hotel) in his first memory. Karina's first memory is of falling off the wall outside the factory where her mother worked. Yet amidst all this distress and misfortune, here is my father's first memory: a tall man arrives to pick him up from a nursery. This is his father, he would learn later, though at the time, he didn't know there was such a thing.

> I remember sitting in the small Ford coupe that was our family car and looking in the back at a bag or a basket of roundish purple things. What are those? I ask. Those are plums. Can I have one? Yes. It squirts delicious juice into my mouth as I take my first bite.